10-8-04

The Farm Welding
Handbook

The Farm Welding
Handbook

Richard Finch

MOTORBOOKS

First published in 2005 by Motorbooks, an imprint of MBI Publishing Company, Galtier Plaza, Suite 200, 380 Jackson Street, St. Paul, MN 55101-3885 USA

The information in this book is true and complete to the best of our knowledge. All recommendations are made without any guarantee on the part of the author or Publisher, who also disclaim any liability incurred in connection with the use of this data or specific details.

This publication has been prepared solely by MBI Publishing Company and is not approved or licensed by any other entity. We recognize that some words, model names, and designations mentioned herein are the property of the trademark holder. We use them for identification purposes only. This is not an official publication.

Motorbooks titles are also available at discounts in bulk quantity for industrial or sales-promotional use. For details write to Special Sales Manager at MBI Publishing Company, Galtier Plaza, Suite 200, 380 Jackson Street, St. Paul, MN 55101-3885 USA.

ISBN-13: 978-0-7603-2251-2
ISBN-10: 0-7603-2251-1

Editorial: Amy Glaser
Design: Christopher Fayers

Printed in China

Front cover: Welding techniques are demonstrated on and around the farm.

Back cover: A southpaw is fusion welding a cluster of steel tubing in this photo. H. G. Frautschy of EAA Oshkosh is practicing his gas welding skills. He is wearing a full number 5 shade face shield over his prescription glasses. The tip cleaner is lying nearby and is ready for use, if needed.

About the author:
Richard Finch is a longtime certified welder and welding consultant to NASA. He also is the author of several other welding books, including *Performance Welding*. He lives in Tularosa, New Mexico, and spends some of his time traveling the country in an RV with his wife.

CONTENTS

Acknowledgments 6

Introduction 6

CHAPTER 1: **Setting Up a Farm Welding Shop** 7

CHAPTER 2: **Farm Welding Safety** 27

CHAPTER 3: **Typical Farm Welding Processes** 34

CHAPTER 4: **Identifying Metals in the Farm Welding Shop** 47

CHAPTER 5: **Oxyacetylene Cutting, Heating, and Plasma Cutting** 52

CHAPTER 6: **Oxyacetylene Welding: Steel, Aluminum, and Stainless** 69

CHAPTER 7: **Arc Welding: AC/DC Current Machines** 81

CHAPTER 8: **MIG Welding, Gas, and Flux Core** 103

CHAPTER 9: **Special Hard-to-Weld Metals** .114

CHAPTER 10: **Where to Buy Welding Supplies** 123

Index 142

ACKNOWLEDGMENTS

The author would like to thank: Craig Massey, Communications Manager, New Mexico Farm and Ranch Heritage Museum; Nancy De Busk, Store Owner, Sears; Dotty Hammack, Branch Manager, Valley Gas and Specialty; Scott Skrjanc, Event Marketing Manager, Lincoln Electric Company; Don Munson, Rocky Mountain Marketing & Sales, Hobart Welders; Mike Pankoratz, Marketing, Miller Electric; Jason and Shannon Woods; Ken Henderson; Norvall Bookout; Leslie Abercrombie; and Gayle Finch.

INTRODUCTION

If you are interested in repairing farm equipment or building implements for the farm, ranch, or vineyard, you will soon discover that almost anybody with the time to read this book and practice various welding projects can become a good welder. For example, several years ago, a farmer in America's breadbasket built an experimental replica of the famous Gee Bee biplane racer and exhibited it at air shows throughout the country. To illustrate what a useful and satisfying avocation welding can be, I've included herein stories and pictures of a variety of people from different age groups.

Not too long ago in the United States, farming was a way of life for most people. If you wanted to eat, you had to work (by farming), as the old saying goes. Today, many people don't have to farm for their food but choose to do so for the enjoyment and satisfaction they get from repairing and building implements, working the land, and reaping the harvest they sowed. To lay the groundwork for welding, repairing, and building farm implements, Chapter 1 offers some highlights from the history of metalworking.

Archeologists use a three-age system to classify the types of tools and weapons used by man. Before the advent of metal, there was the Stone Age. The discovery of metal ushered in the Bronze Age, and the development of iron tools and weapons marked the beginning of the Iron Age.

'ers and manufacturers started producing mechanized farm equipment, such as horse-drawn plows, rakes, planters, cultivators, and many specialized tools to make farming faster, easier, and more profitable. To better illustrate the more recent history of farm implements I will profile in a later chapter the New Mexico Farm and Ranch Heritage Museum, which is located just off Interstate Highway 10 outside of Las Cruces, New Mexico. It's worth a visit if you're in that area.

Even though metal farm implements are rugged and durable, they can easily break if used improperly and—like everything else—they wear out with use. This led to the development of a new type of craftsman: the blacksmith. The term *blacksmith* can be traced to two sources. A person in a trade that made and repaired things was called a smith, and because this particular smith got dirty from the smoke and soot of his trade, he became a "black" smith. Blacksmithing flourished until the advent of arc and oxyacetylene welding. Today, blacksmithing is almost a lost art, having been replaced mostly by local welding shops and portable welding rigs.

Moving beyond the history of metalworking, this book is really a practical manual on how to weld almost anything—and often many more things than the local blacksmith shop could ever do. Thumb through the pages, see what you can learn, and then go out and weld something!

CHAPTER 1
SETTING UP A FARM WELDING SHOP

Once you determine your farm weld shop budget and what kinds of welding you want to do, setting up your shop will be easy. To help you decide how to set up your own shop, we will examine five different rural barns and their welding shops. Keep in mind that you can start off with a simple welding setup and add to it as you see the need for more advanced welding techniques and tools. But first let's take a look at the history of metalworking.

METALWORKING IN THE BRONZE AGE

The Bronze Age began before 3,000 B.C. when humans first discovered that sufficiently heating a specific type of dirt over a period of time created coals with harder, more durable properties than the wood and charcoal that usually came out of the fire.

It was also discovered that gold and silver could be extracted from the ground by heating various kinds of dirt that we now call ore. Then people learned that blowing air through fire would create a hotter fire. Early drawings of furnaces show a hand-pumped bellows, and later drawings depict work animals pulling and pushing a bellows to blow air into furnaces to super-heat the fire. The earliest fires burned wood for fuel, then charcoal was used, followed by coal furnaces, and in our age of steel, oil and natural gas are the most efficient methods to smelt metals from earth ore.

The old building in this picture was, from 1922 until 1956, the Witte Blacksmith Shop in Stanley, New Mexico. It has since been moved to this location at the New Mexico Farm and Ranch Heritage Museum in Las Cruces, New Mexico.

This is the rock slab hearth where the fire was located in the Witte Blacksmith Shop. Charcoal and coal were used to make a very hot fire, and the pipe supplied air to make the fire even hotter. Courtesy of New Mexico Farm and Ranch Heritage Museum

The stand in the center of this picture that looks like a barbecue grill is actually a portable blacksmith hearth. The blower at the right of the hearth is a hand-cranked unit that supplies high-volume air to the coals to make the fire hotter. I spent many childhood days turning a blower wheel just like this to make a hot hearth fire on a farm in Texas. Courtesy of New Mexico Farm and Ranch Heritage Museum

The sign on this building on the grounds of the New Mexico Farm and Ranch Heritage Museum in Las Cruces, New Mexico, says "Blacksmithing." The building houses an authentic antique blacksmith shop with real blacksmith tools and a working hearth with a viewing space for visitors. The beautiful Organ Mountains are in the background.

METALWORKING IN THE IRON AGE

Pig iron and what generally resembles steel was being smelted before 1,000 B.C. Pig iron earned its name because the first iron meltings resembled a piglet. It was later discovered that adding carbon to the iron made the metal much harder and capable of maintaining a sharp edge, which enabled the metalworkers to create swords and plowshares. Iron ore is the fourth most abundant of the Earth's elements. Pure iron melts at 2,795 degrees Fahrenheit and boils at 5,207 degrees Fahrenheit.

METALWORKING IN THE STEEL AGE

In the nineteenth century, Sir Henry Bessemer, a British citizen, discovered and improved the modern process of injecting super-heated air and oxygen into a flame to forge steel. The Bessemer process of open-hearth heating recycles hot air from the exhaust, creating temperatures above 3,000 degrees Fahrenheit. A plain coal flame reaches about 1,000 degrees or less without the addition of hot air.

There are five classes of steel in order of refinement. Carbon steel is used in I-beams, angle iron, and mild-steel sheet metal. Alloy steel is used in car bodies and structural steel. Alloy is the most common form of steel in farm and ranch welding. High-strength steels are used in making knives and gears, and are commonly called low-alloy steel, meaning they contain less than 0.30 percent carbon. Stainless steels are the next higher level of refinement. There are presently over 100 different alloys of stainless steel; some are magnetic, but most are nonmagnetic. Stainless steels are made in electric furnaces instead of open-hearth furnaces. The tool steels, tungsten (the heaviest of all steels) and molybdenum, are the last class. Another metallic substance is mercury (atomic symbol Hg), which melts at minus 39.97 degrees Fahrenheit and boils at 641 degrees Fahrenheit. Mercury is the only metal that is liquid at room temperature.

9

The man in this replica blacksmith shop is Ben LoBue, a blacksmith for the New Mexico Farm and Ranch Heritage Museum. LoBue owns a blacksmith company called A Mountain Forge, but he also does blacksmithing demonstrations at the museum. Steel and iron implements that Ben makes in this blacksmith shop are for sale in the museum gift shop. The required air blower is actually an electric blower that is located in the wood box to the right of the stone hearth.

Ben LoBue hammers a piece of red-hot steel rod on a heavy cast-steel anvil to form the end of the rod into a flat shape. The rod will soon become a tool for a fireplace set. The primary tools for the blacksmith are a 4-pound hammer, a 90-pound anvil, and the fire in the hearth. Blacksmiths could do wonders with cold steel once they heated it in the hearth. New Mexico Farm and Ranch Heritage Museum

This complicated steel structure is the tongue assembly for a horse-drawn road grader that was built in the mid-1920s. It shows some recent welding as a modification for use with a steam-powered tractor, but note the large number of rivets in the assembly. It was much easier for a blacksmith shop to pierce hot steel and install hot rivets than it was to forge weld the same structure. New Mexico Farm and Ranch Heritage Museum

THE ERA OF THE BLACKSMITH

The era of the blacksmith has definitely come and gone, and most remaining blacksmith shops are now welding shops. As a matter of fact, much of America's steel production has ceased and has moved to other countries, including China, India, and Mexico. But it will still be helpful to take a brief look at a blacksmith shop from a bygone era.

AIR-ASSISTED HEATING

The primary function of a blacksmith shop is to heat steel to the point where it could be easily formed by twisting or hammering over a large cast-steel anvil. When steel is heated to a bright scaling red, it becomes very soft and easy to bend, stretch, or twist with hand tools. Steel melts at 2,500 to 2,786 degrees Fahrenheit. A blacksmith hearth usually reaches no more than 1,725 degrees Fahrenheit, which turns steel orange. Just barely red or faint red is only 900 degrees Fahrenheit. Blood-red steel is 1,050 degrees

Fahrenheit, and the best temperature for forming steel in a blacksmith hearth is 1,550 degrees Fahrenheit. A coal or charcoal fire without injected air reaches less than 900 degrees Fahrenheit. Before the advent of electricity, air was forced through coals by hand turning a blower similar in design to a modern turbocharger fan and housing, but less efficient.

BLACKSMITH SHOP OPERATIONS

When steel is heated to 1,725 degrees, Fahrenheit, it becomes possible to punch holes through it with a cold chisel or punch. Heated rivets could then be inserted through beams to provide structural support for buildings and other structures. Smaller holes could also be punched through steel horseshoes so they could be nailed directly to the horse's hoof. Horseshoe nails were made from steel wire and were heated and formed to the shape of a nail.

But in farm country, the major use of the blacksmith's forge was to heat plow points and add new metal to the worn areas at the front of plows. This welding was accomplished

Gayle Finch discusses a planned horseshoeing with a ranch hand at the Tularosa, New Mexico, thoroughbred farm owned by Robert and Brandy Samuell. The farm uses welded pipe corrals (shown in the background). The black GMC pickup replaces the horse-drawn farrier's (horseshoeing) wagon and portable hearth. Blacksmithing and horseshoeing have come a long, long way.

by heating the steel plow and the piece of steel patch material to the maximum forge temperature and then adding borax to clean the steel parts. The borax acted like a flux and protected the hot parts so they could be hammer welded into one piece. Old, efficient blacksmith shops had belt-driven drop hammers that fused the steel parts together. The belt was usually driven by a waterwheel or by human power. And, of course, horses, mules, and oxen were also used to drive the shaft that turned the belt. As metallurgical science progressed, elements were added to make a hard facing material that lasted much longer for plowing fields than the old softer mild steel. For current methods and materials for hard facing wear surfaces on plows, dozer blades, and similar steel parts, refer to Chapters 6 and 7.

MODERN BLACKSMITH OPERATIONS

There's a trend today to go back to making driveway gates, steel patio furniture, and decorative items with ornamental iron, which is really mild steel or cast iron. Natural gas

furnaces, which are fired by injecting large amounts of air to raise the temperature of the flame, are the best way to produce the heat needed to bend these steel parts. The same work could be done with an oxyacetylene torch, but the quantity of oxygen and acetylene gasses needed would be prohibitively expensive.

MODERN-DAY HORSESHOEING

Making horseshoes to fit each individual horse was once common. Straps of steel stock were heated in a forge and formed to fit the horse's hoof. Each fitting meant that the hot shoe had to be cooled in water before it was tested for a good fit. Today, pre-fitted horseshoes are the norm. Most farriers (person who shoes horses) now use a cold-fitting method, but they also use an oxyacetylene torch to heat and bend each horseshoe. Farriers used to travel around the country with portable blacksmith shops in the back of horse-drawn wagons. Today, farriers travel around the country in new air-conditioned pickup trucks.

Tony Savalo and his wife get ready to put new shoes on Trixie, a two-year-old thoroughbred. Tony uses a very modern set of farrier tools and only resorts to heat when the horse's hooves need special shoes to fit properly. If pre-made shoes don't fit well, Tony uses an oxyacetylene torch to heat and bend the steel shoes.

Off with the old shoes, on with the new. The new shoes are on the left, and the old shoes are on the right, except for one shoe that's still on the horse. No heat was needed to fit the new shoes, and they fit like a glove. In the past, each shoe was custom formed by heating steel strap material in a blacksmith forge.

This is an authentic New Mexico pole barn that was built by welding steel pipe to a steel roof structure. The poles are set in concrete, and the roof is welded to each pole. This pole barn required quite a bit of overhead welding. The chilies hanging from the roof rails are being dried and prepared for sale. In the background, you can see an old Farmall tractor and a cultivator.

Jason and Shannon Woods own this very well-equipped barn workshop located about 4 miles west of the town of Alamogordo, New Mexico. The dune buggy in the picture was built by Jason, who used his tube-bending tool. The buggy frame was welded with a Hobart 250-amp wire-feed machine. This shop even has a bathroom.

Jason Woods stands in front of his very full Craftsman rollaway toolbox and the wood drawers where he stores additional tools, including a gas welding set, paint spray guns, and more hand tools. From the sign on the wall, Woods appears to be partial to Chevy Trucks.

EXAMPLES OF BARNS AND SHOPS

To illustrate different types of welding shops, we'll now profile five rural barns and workshops. We'll see the simplicity of a shop in a pole barn and the broad-range usefulness of a very well-equipped shop. You'll need to decide how much time and money you want to spend to equip your own shop. The shop with the simplest range of equipment was built with a pickup-truck-mounted arc welder and gas-welding rig. The best equipped shop actually rivals many modern auto and tractor repair shops.

Thoroughbred Farm Barn

The welding equipment in a typical barn consists of a Miller Bobcat 250-amp rig, an oxyacetylene cutting torch, and a 4-inch angle guider and a cut-off saw. The primary purpose of the welding equipment is to build pipe corrals and do maintenance welding around the farm. Other welded items include a racing gate to help train future racehorses how to "beat 'em out of the gate."

New Mexico Pole Barn

In the Southwest, farmers have long known that they don't really need walls on their barns. Just a few pipes or wood poles to hold up the roof will do just fine. The primary purpose of an open pole barn is to have a roof to keep thunderstorms and the occasional snowstorm off the equipment and crops stored there. Having no walls actually helps keep the crops dry and clean.

This pole barn was built with a portable gasoline-powered 250-amp Lincoln welding rig that was borrowed from a brother-in-law. No welding equipment is kept here. Any welding repairs are done in the field by borrowing the family gasoline-generator welding rig.

Factory-Built Workshop

The factory-built workshop is very up-to-date and has a lot of equipment. It was built to be used as a hobby shop, but it's also used to repair and build farm equipment. About the only tool missing from this shop is a hoist for cars and

Ken Henderson did such a professional job building his pole barn that it looks like a steel factory kit, which it isn't. The barn is located about 12 miles south of Alamogordo, New Mexico, at an altitude of 4,200 feet above sea level. The Sacramento Mountains, seen behind the barn, are 9,200 feet above sea level. This barn is located on Henderson's horse farm and vineyard. The barn is still a work in progress, and Henderson is planning interior improvements.

Ken Henderson and his dog show off his collector VW Beetle. Before Henderson can do any welding in the barn, he will need to clean up the area, put up a spark-proof curtain in front of the haystack, and sweep the floor. He will also need to have fire extinguishers and water buckets handy.

This typical Midwestern all-wood barn was built in 1916 with a concrete floor and a wooden floor in the loft. The barn's wood construction could prove to be a hazardous location for a welding shop, but one could be set up with careful planning. The best way to protect this wood structure would be to completely line a separate room on the concrete floor with metal walls and ceiling so sparks and flames couldn't start a fire.

trucks, and one could be installed if needed. There is even a bathroom off the main shop, and the owner, Jason Woods, only has to go into the house to eat and sleep! Woods even has an electronic engine tune-up machine in his shop. For a comprehensive list of Woods' tools, see the chart in this chapter.

Another Pole Barn

This shop looks like a steel frame factory from the outside, but once inside you can see that it has a frame of old telephone poles and heavy lumber. It's a tribute to the craftsmanship that the steel siding is so straight. The owner, Ken Henderson, is slowly building a vineyard and horse ranch. He has no electricity and has to use a gasoline-powered generator for welding and for tools that need 110- and 220-volt power. The barn is a combination unit that does triple duty as a hay barn, horse stable, and workshop. Henderson will soon run 220-volt power in a buried trench that runs about ¼ mile to the nearest power source. Henderson also

has room to build a dirt runway for airplanes. The runway will be covered with wood chips from the local Mescalero Apache Indian Tribe's sawmill.

The welding equipment in Henderson's barn includes a nearly new Lincoln Square Wave TIG/stick welder and an oxyacetylene rig. He also has an air force surplus 110- and 220-volt trailer-mounted motor generator and numerous shop tools, such as a heavy-duty floor-mount drill press, grinding tools, and bench grinders.

Converted Storage Room

In the converted storage room, I took a 16x20-foot storage room and converted it to a workshop, welding shop, and welding-school classroom. I would also like to use it to restore antique cars and airplanes. The shop is powered by a 50-amp 220-volt circuit and has air-conditioning and electric heat. This shop is equipped with tools from over 60 years of hobby work, and purchasing and using these tools helped me make a living. If a tool is worth buying, it is

Yes, this Kohler generator is covered with New Mexico desert dust, but it is powered by a Perkins diesel engine—a pretty good piece of equipment for a farm welding shop, especially one without electricity. The generator is an air force surplus unit and was picked up for a song at a local air base auction. Just blow the dust off, change the engine oil, give it a diesel tune-up, and it should be ready to make a lot of electricity.

The corner of Ken Henderson's pole barn shows the actual telephone pole that supports the roof, the 2x8-inch boards that the steel walls attach to, and the storage area for an air compressor and gas-welding cart. Look closely at the picture of the barn's exterior to appreciate how well it's built.

This corner of Ken Henderson's pole-barn workshop has a set of steel shelves where Henderson plans to set up his TIG welding shop. The oxyacetylene welding rig is next to the wood pole and behind the steel shelves. The shelves were purchased at an auction at Holloman Air Force Base, New Mexico.

This is the welding area in the author's workshop. Note that it's mostly white for better lighting and visibility while welding. The handiest thing in the whole shop is the welding/cutting table on wheels. The cutting area is closed in on four sides and the bottom to catch sparks and slag. The kitchen stool is just the right height for sitting while welding.

An assortment of metal clamps used for tack welding hang on the pegboard. Some clamps have plastic tips to prevent marring painted surfaces. The handiest of all are the big clothespin-type metal clamps.

Every welding shop should have an assortment of grinders and cut-off wheel tools. The 4-inch grinder on the right was on sale in a mail-order catalog for only $9.95. It should last for at least 5 years. Note the abrasive flap wheel at the top. It's 80-grit abrasive and will do a better job than typical grinding stones.

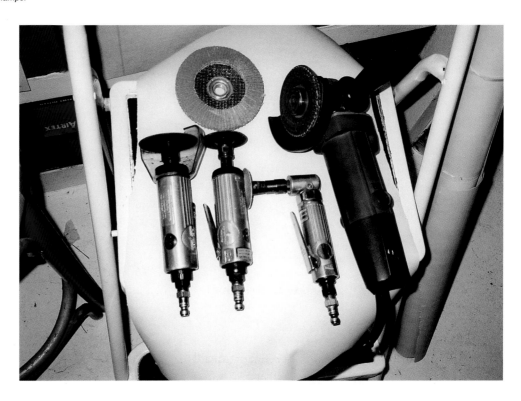

This band saw has been slowed down to a ratio of 34 to 1. The 1,725-rpm motor is still turning the same speed, but the band saw's blade wheels now only turn at 50 rpm. That speed works well for sawing steel with 18- to 24-teeth-per-inch blades. The sprockets also allow for a 3.4 to 1 ratio for sawing aluminum castings with 12- to 18-teeth-per-inch blades, and a 2.0 to 1 ratio for sawing wood. You will have to buy your own chain, sprockets, bearings, and shafts to make your own reduction ratios.

The tools in Jason Woods' shop include:

- Floor-mounted Pro-Tools tubing bender
- Floor drill press
- Floor band saw capable of cutting metal
- Propane shop heater
- Miller Pro-Cut plasma cutting machine
- Allen Computer Tester tune-up machine
- Honda pressure washer (2,750 psi)
- Craftsman 14-inch metal-cutting chop saw
- Lincoln 225-amp buzzbox arc welder
- Hobart Beta MIG 250-amp with spool gun for aluminum
- Solvent parts washer tank and drum of solvent
- Bucket sand blaster
- Air compressor (7 1/2 horsepower, 220 volt, 80 gallon, 30 cfm at 90 psi)
- Corrosive storage cabinet
- Bryant 120,000-Btu forced-air ceiling heater
- Engine chain hoist
- Engine overhaul stand
- Large portable floor fan
- HVLP (high-volume, low-pressure) spray-paint gun
- Metal-halide (250-watt) T4 portable lights, General Electric mercury-vapor lights

There are hand tools, especially air tools, too numerous to list. The shop measures 30x40 feet and has 1,200 square feet of floor space and a very high ceiling. There are many different ways to equip your farm welding shop. It's up to you to do what is most economically efficient for your own situation and farm needs. A number of other tools you may want to buy are listed in this chapter.

worth keeping. The welding equipment in the shop consists of nearly all "red" equipment: Lincoln Electric Welders. The welders include a Lincoln Square Wave 175 TIG and stick machine, a Lincoln Invertec V205T AC/DC TIG and stick machine that weighs only 38 pounds and runs on 110 or 220 volts, an SP-125 Plus MIG welder, and a Pro-Cut 25 plasma cutter that also runs on either 110 or 220 volts.

In addition to numerous hand and power tools, the shop is also equipped with gas welding equipment including a Harris torch and cutting head, another smaller and portable Harris torch, a Dillon pistol-grip torch and cutting head, a Smiths aircraft torch, and a BernzOmatic MAPP gas and oxygen torch. The shop is also equipped with a metal-cutting band saw, a floor-model drill press, and a combination metal lathe and milling machine.

You could make your own farm equipment with the technology in this shop, and several national class-winning race cars and several experimental airplanes have actually been created in this shop.

TOOLS TO BUY FOR YOUR FARM SHOP
This list is more or less in the order of importance.
- A good, large bench vise that weighs about 50 pounds and has jaws that open to 8 inches is a lifetime investment. Everything you work on will need to be held in a good vise at one time or another. Don't scrimp, buy the best vise you can find.

This inexpensive bench grinder now has an 80-grit abrasive flap wheel on one side and a wire wheel on the other side. Abrasive flap wheels have made the old-style grinding wheels almost obsolete. Make sure the plastic eye guards are left in place.

The 14-inch cut-off saw in this picture only cost $70 from a mail-order catalog. It works great for cutting any steel, including angle, tubing, and solid rods. It will not work for sawing aluminum because aluminum will clog the blade and cause it to break. Use a band or skill saw to cut aluminum angle, tubing, and rods.

- An air compressor is a necessary shop tool. Do not be tempted to buy one of the $100 diaphragm units. It will never be useful, and you will soon be shopping for a better one if you buy a cheap one first. The minimum-quality air compressor you should buy is a two-cylinder piston compressor with an air tank as big as you can fit into your shop. And as a matter of fact, consider putting the air compressor in a separate room outside your shop so the noise won't be bothersome. Once you have the compressor, you can stock up on air tools. They'll make your life much easier.

- Various air tools will be very handy. Discount mail-order catalogs sell some small cut-off tools for under $10. Buy several and keep them ready for use with grinders, cut-off wheels, wire brushes, and sanders already installed. Or make a list and give your friends and relatives something to put in your Christmas stocking every year.

- Sandblasting cabinets can save a lot of time and make repair jobs go a lot faster. A small bucket-type sand-blaster is better than sandpaper, but a really nice cabinet will make your life a lot easier and cleaner. You can even use the sandblasting cabinet to remove old paint and rust from parts before welding.

- You should place several fire extinguishers in strategic locations around your shop. You can buy dry-chemical fire extinguishers at the local discount store for under $10 apiece. Also, you should have about five 5-gallon buckets ready to fill with water if you have a small fire.

A FARRIER'S TALE

As Richard's wife and photography assistant over the years, I've had the good fortune to meet some interesting people. South-central New Mexico is the home of the richest purses in quarter-horse racing. At Ruidoso, New Mexico, the million-dollar futurity is run every Labor Day at the racetrack in Ruidoso Downs. In a racing season that runs from spring to Labor Day, appendix registry quarter horses race others in their age range or in open competition for purses among the richest in the country.

Recently we were privileged to visit a specialized type of ranching operation that includes the breeding of running quarter-horse and thoroughbred stock, along with the facilities of their housing and training while these horses are turned into racing machines, sometimes prior to their actual second birthdays.

We drove to Horseman's Park, a place just north of Tularosa, New Mexico, where Robert and Brandy Samuell buy and sell racing stock and break and train horses to become racehorses. We had an appointment with Tony Savalo of Glencoe, New Mexico, a farrier and a specialist in both normal horseshoeing and remedial, or corrective, shoeing. We were privileged to watch Tony "cold shoe" (without using a heat-treated shoeing process) a two-year-old black thoroughbred filly named Trixie. This was probably Trixie's second or third experience of being shod, and she pawed and snorted, which required Tony's wife to assist in calming her so the shoeing could proceed.

The facilities for training and raising these animal athletes have undergone a modernization since I was involved in raising hobby and show stock quarter horses some 30 years ago. I can appreciate how much mechanized equipment and training techniques have eased the workload in this very specialized kind of ranching, but it remains a tough way to make a living. I really admire the Samuell family, Tony Savalo, the trainers, and all the people involved in this kind of ranching.

—Gayle Finch

This Miller Bobcat 225-amp generator welder is used by Pueblo Pipe and Steel for projects. It will soon be installed in the trailer project shown in Chapter 7, making it completely portable. It can also be used as a power supply for other electrical shop equipment such as grinders, MIG welders, and air compressors. Pueblo Pipe and Steel

Buy a good garden hose and have it ready to put out smoldering embers.

- Fire-resistant metal cabinets are necessary to store your paint. Put your grease gun in there, too. If you have paint cans in your shop, you don't want them exposed to welding sparks.
- Here is what you should look for in welding equipment. Always buy the big heavy-capacity machine. A 350-amp arc welder is much better than an 80-amp machine, but you may not need any more than 250 amps in a stick welding machine. A 175-amp MIG welder is about the minimum size for farm welding, but a 200-amp MIG machine is even better. The little 100-amp machines will only weld fenders and lawn mowers, not trailers and tractors.
- Oxyacetylene rigs are a necessity. You can buy a complete rig with tanks for about $500. You will need to

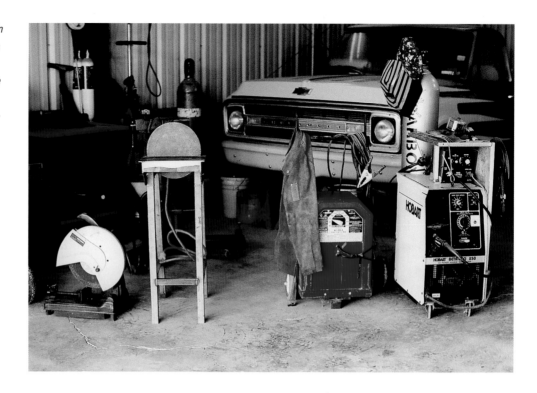

This is some of the equipment in Jason Woods' shop. From left to right: A solvent parts washer, a cut-off wheel saw, a homemade 1½-horsepower sanding disc, a 225-amp Lincoln buzzbox stick-welding machine, a 250-amp Hobart wire-feed welder, and a Chevy pickup project vehicle. Jason Woods

Another shot of Jason Woods' shop shows the bathroom to the left. In the picture are also the floor-model drill press, the floor-model band saw, a Miller stick welder, an Allen computer tune-up test machine, a Honda pressure washer, and a homemade 1 1/2-horsepower sander. This could easily be a commercial fabrication shop. Jason Woods

cut, heat, and bend before you can weld, so plan on a good medium-size gas-welding rig. Even a medium-size gas welder can solder and braze. And you'll learn here how to use it for everything from cutting 1-inch-thick steel to soldering a fitting on your tractor radiator.

• Hand tools are a given necessity. You will need a set of ⅜-inch-drive sockets and ratchets, a set of ½-inch-drive sockets and ratchets, and maybe even a larger set of ¾-inch-drive sockets. Don't be tempted to buy one of the super-cheap, large-quantity, poor-quality tool sets. Go to your local Sears store and buy a set of Craftsman tools or purchase the more expensive Snap-on tools. Mac brand tools are good, too. If you're bored on Saturday mornings, you can go to swap meets and find high-quality used tools at good prices.

In many of the pictures in this book, you will see the snowcapped 12,000-foot Sierra Blanca Mountain in the background. The mountain is the dominant scene in this part of New Mexico because it rises from a 4,500-foot desert floor. In this picture, taken from Highway 54-70, the mountain is about 22 miles away.

Jason Woods makes good use of this Pro-Tools pipe and tubing bender to bend 1- to 2-inch tubing for a number of projects, including roll bars and pickup racks. See Chapter 2 for another kind of tubing bender that does not work as well. Jason Woods

• There are a few brands to consider when buying welders. Some people swear by the "red" welders (Lincoln Electric), some swear by the "blue" welders (Miller Electric), and others swear by the "brown" welders (Hobart). All three brands are of high quality, but the main thing is to buy your equipment from a dealer that offers good service. Don't buy a welder if there's no dealer for it in your area. What if you need a part on Friday afternoon? Make sure your dealer can meet all of your welding needs.

Cronatron Welding Systems, Inc., makes this large clamp for outside objects. It can also be reversed to clamp or provide pressure from inside objects. Tool courtesy of Cronatron Welding Systems, Inc.

This large magnetic clamp can be turned on and off by flipping the red switch on its side. It works great for clamping round, angle, or flat steel. It has a very strong magnet that will hold even large structures for tack welding. Tool courtesy of Cronatron Welding Systems, Inc.

Sometimes it's OK to weld without gloves for more accuracy, but once your hands get hot you can't do an accurate job. It's best to have some clean new gloves on hand. The blue pair of gloves is for arc and MIG welding and some gas welding. The white Cronatron gloves on the right are made of soft, pliable deerskin for delicate welding and soldering, and they're especially great for TIG welding. Gloves courtesy of Cronatron Welding Systems, Inc.

CHAPTER 2
FARM WELDING SAFETY

"**B**arn burning" is a phrase used in many farming communities to mean that something is really exciting. But we don't want your building to actually burn down, so we need to discuss how to prevent your barn or workshop from catching fire while you're welding.

EXCLUDE FLAMMABLES

First of all, you want to make sure that your welding area is clear of flammable materials. This is most important in a farm workshop where there's usually hay, feed, seed sacks, and fertilizer sacks scattered around. Take some time and clean your work area. This includes getting rid of grass, tree leaves, scrap lumber, and old storage boxes. Take a look at the old barn in the photo on this page. If you were to strike an arc in this barn, you might as well call the volunteer fire department. Clean the place up before you burn it down!

SPARK CONTAINMENT

One of the best ways to contain sparks is very easy. An old 55-gallon barrel with the top cut out is good for containing sparks from cutting and welding operations. Another way to contain sparks is to build a combination welding and cutting table with wheels mounted on one side. Put handles on the cart so you can move it around the shop and even outside. You won't get much sleep if you lay awake at night wondering if the sparks that flew all over the shop earlier in the day have smoldered into a fire. You'll sleep a lot better if you know that the sparks were safely contained in

If your barn is as cluttered as this one, you need to spend some time clearing out all the weeds and brush. And don't forget the straw and hay in the barn. Trying to weld in a barn like this would be asking for a barn burning. It's absolutely critical that you rid out all flammables before you start to weld.

Sparks from plasma cutting this piece of ¼-inch steel plate can start a fire, even several minutes after the cutting operation is over. Don't let sparks fly near flammables, like under your wood workbench.

a metal container. One hint for building a cutting table is to go to you local metal supply dealer and buy a sheet of ¼-inch expanded metal and lay it on the cutting barrel or box. If after several years it becomes cut up and ratty, you can replace it with another sheet.

EXPLOSION HAZARDS

It might seem like a good idea to take that empty 55-gallon oil drum and make a barbecue grill out of it. The problem with simply attacking it with a cutting torch is that it likely still has flammable fumes in it that could explode as soon as the cutting torch pierces the drum. Even barrels or drums that have had floor wax in them can explode with disastrous results from fumes inside the container.

A safer way to make a barbecue grill is to fill the drum with water and use your cutting torch to cut the top seam first. One very hazardous way to cut a drum has caused many deaths from explosions. Here it is: Old timers may tell you to put the tailpipe of your car into the bung and run the engine exhaust gas into the tank to "purge" it. Car exhaust still has lots of explosive vapor and unburned fuel left in it, and the "purged" barrel or tank can explode when the flame of the torch comes in contact with the exhaust gas.

CARRYING OXYGEN AND ACETYLENE TANKS

It's generally safe to carry a full or empty oxygen tank in a closed area, such as the trunk of a car, because if the tank should leak, oxygen will not burn by itself. But if an acetylene tank leaks in a closed area like the trunk of a car, it becomes a potential bomb if it's ignited by a spark. Acetylene tanks are full of acetone saturated fiber, plus the acetylene, and they should never be laid on their sides. Keep the acetylene tank upright at all times. So it's safer to chain or strap the tanks to the side of a pickup or trailer to transport them. See Chapter 6 for more information on gas welding tanks.

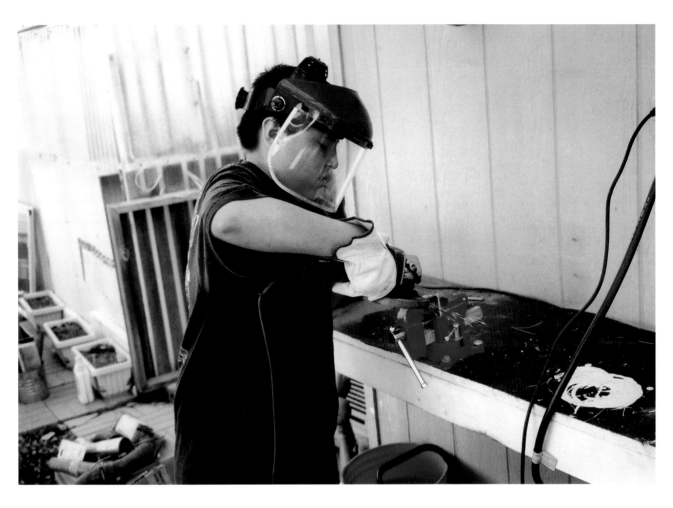

Here, 11-year-old Dimetras Rocha is using a 4-inch grinder to knock slag off a piece of ¼-inch steel plate. This kind of grinding creates fewer sparks than a cutting torch or a plasma torch but still makes sparks that start fires. Be alert and aware of where your sparks fly.

An old 55-gallon oil drum like this can make a good barbecue grill, but it can also kill you while you're cutting it to make the grill. If you don't purge the explosive vapors from the drum prior to plasma or gas torch cutting, the drum could explode as soon as you start to cut it open. Filling it with water keeps the vapors from exploding while you cut it open.

These oxygen and acetylene tanks will last for several days, weeks, or months of welding and cutting, then you'll need to transport them to a welding gas dealer to be refilled or exchanged for full tanks. Don't ever carry acetylene tanks in the closed trunk of your car! A leaking valve on the acetylene tank could cause an explosion.

STORING FLAMMABLES

One thing that's caused many fires and explosions in welding shops and areas is a can of paint or paint thinner sitting nearby. Just one spark or arc from a welding torch or arc welder can set off a fire or explosion just as surely as a bomb can be set off by a lit fuse. It's inevitable that you'll have flammable materials in your welding area at one time or another, but be sure to protect them from ignition sources.

One farm welding shop owner has found a very good surplus steel cabinet to store his paints, thinners, cleaning solvents, and other flammables. The primary thing is to make sure that sparks can't get to your flammables. This includes storing your oily, greasy rags in a steel can with a steel lid.

Jason Woods bought this corrosives cabinet at a surplus sale at a nearby air force base. He has another cabinet like this for flammables. Welding sparks will not get into these steel cabinets.

New Mexico horse rancher and vineyard owner Ken Henderson will need to clean up this future welding shop area in his pole barn before he makes sparks here. The wooden poles could also be flammable and should be wrapped in sheet metal to prevent a fire.

STORING ACIDS

An excellent rust remover is a mix of phosphoric acid and water. Keep a spray bottle of this mix in the weld shop area to quickly and easily remove rust before you weld steel or cast iron. Just spray the mix on a rusty piece of steel about 30 minutes prior to cutting and welding, and the rust magically disappears. But before you cut or weld the once rusty piece of metal, rinse it off in clear water to neutralize the acid. If you try cutting or welding acid-covered metal, the fumes from the acid will be very hazardous to your nose, mouth, throat, and eyes. Rust is the process of iron and steel oxidizing back into its natural state. Phosphoric acid works to remove or neutralize rust by converting it back to oxygen and hydrogen. The fumes from the phosphoric acid and water mix are pretty strong, and they can also cause skin burns if you have a break in the skin, so put the corrosives in a cabinet like the one shown in this chapter.

CLEAN UP THE WELDING AREA

In the pole barn shown in this chapter, Ken Henderson has not yet cleaned up his welding area in his dusty new barn. If sparks were to roll under equipment stored in the weld shop area (which they will), they could sit and smolder for several hours and cause a fire. Even a wooden workbench could be the source of spark-caused fires. If necessary, buy a few fire blankets to cover things in your weld shop to prevent sparks from being a hazard.

FACE AND EYE PROTECTION

The most likely physical dangers in a farm weld shop are from things that get into your eyes and hit your face. This makes a full face shield an excellent piece of safety equipment. Grinding wheels can explode if they're stressed beyond reason. Sticking a long pipe or angle steel into a grinding wheel can cause the wheels to burst from being

Dimetras Rocha has bent a piece of ¾-inch black pipe in this hydraulic bender. He's using a clear face shield to protect his eyes and face from splinters from the bending pipe and hydraulic fluid if the jack should burst. The bender collapsed the pipe rather than making a smooth bend.

over-stressed. A good face shield is necessary, and sturdy denim clothing will protect your arms, legs, and torso from injury. The light from gas welding and cutting flames won't burn your eyes, but the arc from MIG welding and the arc from stick or arc welding can cause severe radiation burns to your eyes. Radiation burns from arc welding are similar to a severe sunburn, and your eyes are very susceptible to being burned by the radiation from arc welding. We humans know when our eyes are burning and itching, but our farm animals can't tell us if their eyes are in severe pain, so protect all your farm animals from eye burns from arc-welding rays. Place shields around the area where you need to weld. A simple piece of plywood will often make a good temporary light shield. Dark-green opaque plastic arc-welding curtains are also available through your local welding supply dealer.

FIRST-AID KITS

Every farm welding shop should have a first-aid kit within easy reach of anyone in the shop. The first-aid kit should have burn ointment and eye drops, a few large Band-Aids, and supplies for any weld shop emergency. Make sure that your first-aid kit has fresh supplies that aren't old and dried out. A good brand of hand cleaner is important, too, because you'll need to wash your hands before you apply a Band-Aid on a small cut or scrape.

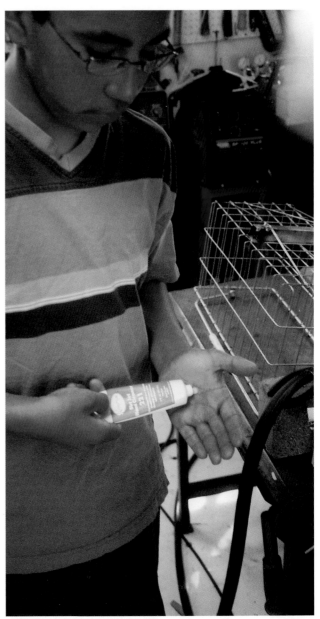

Fourteen-year-old Gregg Rocha is using some Cronatron hand cleaner after brazing a wire basket. It's critical that you keep a well-stocked first-aid kit in your welding shop.

This hay barn is very dry and flammable. It could be cleaned up to be used as a farm weld shop, but another less flammable barn would be safer. The weeds around this barn should be cut, and the hay should be moved. Covering the hay would still be unsafe.

FIRE EXTINGUISHERS

A garden hose is an important safety item in a farm welding shop. A fresh tub of clear water is handy for cooling hot parts, and it could be handy if you have a small fire to extinguish. Standard 2½-pound dry-chemical fire extinguishers are inexpensive at around $10 each. You should have at least one extinguisher at each welding machine and one near the door of your shop. Dry-chemical extinguishers contain a baking soda-type white powder that smothers the fire, but they always leave a messy powdery residue.

BREATHING WELDING FUMES

Due to the very nature of welding, you will always have to contend with toxic fumes. Ordinary safety measures will take care of these hazards, but the welder must be aware of how to avoid breathing bad air. In all kinds of welding, including gas, and especially arc, smoke and fumes will be emitted by the metal parts being welded.

The easiest way to avoid breathing toxic welding fumes is to keep your head out of the smoke that comes from welding. The smoke and fumes from arc welding are very obvious and can usually be avoided if you weld in an open area. But if you are welding in a small, closed shop in the winter without fresh air, you must provide ventilation. The best way to do this is to have a suction fan and a flexible hose that you can place where it's most needed, at the weld.

All of the commercial welding supply companies sell suction fans for welding. In a pinch, you can make your own suction by attaching an 8- to 12-inch-diameter flexible hose to the suction side of a shop fan. The flex hose should be put near the actual weld joint so it can vacuum up the weld smoke and fumes. Of course, the exhaust side of the suction must be vented outside and not into the shop. In cold winter months, you will need to have a damper door on the exhaust side of the fan so cold air won't come into the shop.

CHAPTER 3
TYPICAL FARM WELDING PROCESSES

WHICH PROCESS DO I USE?

In this chapter, we'll discuss the operation of four different welding and cutting processes: oxyacetylene, arc, MIG, and plasma. We'll cover which process best is suited for each type of repair and project you'll want to do on the farm. Knowing which welding and cutting process is most suitable for any given project is the first step to becoming a good welder.

GAS WELDING

If you can only afford one piece of welding equipment, the gas welder (oxyacetylene) is the primary welding tool for all shops. Depending on the size of torch you have, it's possible to gas weld steel as thick as ¾-inch and as thin as 0.010-inch. A simple gas welder with a cutting torch attachment can sever or pierce steel up to 6 inches thick. With careful handling, it is possible to solder a piece of copper tubing to a soft drink can, using a specific alloy of lead solder and special flux (see Chapter 9). It's also possible to braze very thick cast-iron parts, such as an engine block on a tractor.

To build a trailer from angle steel, first cut the exact lengths of steel for the frame and its sides and axles. The gas welder with a cutting attachment does this job very well. In certain cases where a moderate amount of heat is required, the cutting torch can put out enough heat to bend the steel.

Some of the heating jobs are:
- Thawing frozen water pipes
- Heating steel for bending
- Pre-heating thick steel before arc welding

THREE STATES OF ALL MATTER

Processed, manufactured metal is present in three states. The first and coldest state of metal is frozen. That's the piece of metal lying on the shop floor ready to be cut and welded. The next state of metal is liquid. That state is when the foundry made the piece of steel laying on the floor. The piece of steel becomes liquid again when it's cut with a cutting torch and when it is turned into a vapor, the last state of metal. Vaporization can happen whenever you get the metal too hot with a gas welding torch or when you cut it with a cutting torch. Each type of metal has its own freezing point, melting point, and vaporization point. Some of the various farm metals and their three states of temperatures are:

- Aluminum—Freezing point: 1,217 degrees Fahrenheit; Melting point: 1,217 degrees Fahrenheit; Vapor point: 4,442 degrees Fahrenheit
- Brass—Freezing point: 1,652 degrees Fahrenheit; Melting point: 1,652 degrees Fahrenheit; Vapor point: 3,857 degrees Fahrenheit
- Cast Iron—Freezing point: 2,786 degrees Fahrenheit; Melting point: 2,786 degrees Fahrenheit; Vapor point: 5,340 degrees Fahrenheit
- Steel—Freezing point: 2,462 degrees Fahrenheit; Melting point: 2,462 degrees Fahrenheit: Vapor point: 5,450 degrees Fahrenheit

Just think of water, which freezes and melts at 32 degrees Fahrenheit and boils at 212 degrees Fahrenheit at sea level. Metals act the same way.

What this means to the farm welder is that you have to be aware that you can burn up or vaporize your welding project if you don't pay careful attention to how you apply heat. The flame of the gas welding torch is about 6,200 degrees Fahrenheit and can vaporize any of the metals listed in the chart above. The arc welding puddle is usually about 10,000 degrees Fahrenheit.

Plasma cutting temperatures can reach over 50,000 degrees Fahrenheit when cutting. That's why plasma cutting torches will cut any conductive metal, including aluminum, steel, brass, and lead. Plasma is an artificial, not natural, temperature, and that is why the new science books call it the fourth state of matter.

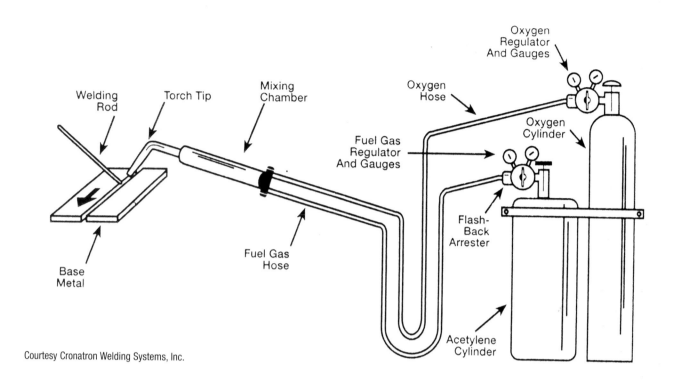

Welding Rod

Torch Tip

Mixing Chamber

Oxygen Hose

Oxygen Regulator And Gauges

Fuel Gas Regulator And Gauges

Oxygen Cylinder

Base Metal

Fuel Gas Hose

Flash-Back Arrester

Acetylene Cylinder

Courtesy Cronatron Welding Systems, Inc.

Separate hoses carry the gases to the torch. The torch has two needle valves. One valve contros the flowr rate of oxygen; the other controls the flow rate of acetylene to the torch mixing chamber. The mixed gases ignited by external means burn at the torch tip. The type and intensity of the flame is adjustable based on the oxygen and acetylene mixture.

This broken plastic handle on a yard cart has been reinforced by oxyacetylene brazing with galvanized steel reinforcement plates brazed to a piece of galvanized electrical tubing. Be very careful not to breathe the toxic fumes from heated galvanized steel. Chapter 6 describes the brazing process.

Farrier Tony Savalo straightens a new horseshoe without using heat. If the shoes need extra bending, Savalo uses an oxyacetylene torch rather than a forge to make the steel shoe bend easily.

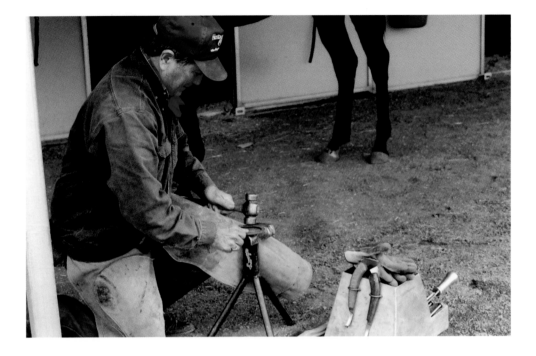

Irrigation pipe like this is usually made from aluminum tubing. The aluminum is often damaged by rough use or by accidents and can be saved from the scrap pile by welding with an oxyacetylene torch or arc welder using flux-core or flux-covered aluminum rod. Chapters 6 and 9 demonstrate how to weld thin aluminum.

- Taking old equipment apart for salvage
- Cutting off rusty nuts and bolts
- Soldering several kinds of metals
- Brazing many kinds of metals
- Fusion welding steel and aluminum

THE OXYACETYLENE PROCESS

When the two gasses are mixed in the brass torch body and set aflame, they can produce a flame with a temperature of about 6,200 degrees Fahrenheit in the small inner flame cone. The heat from this flame cone is able to melt steel at a distance of around 1 inch. The welder is able to play the heat from the flame to reach the desired melting temperature of steel, aluminum, or brazing material to produce a fusion weld or brazed joint. The welder must be well trained in order to produce a sound weld, but a beginning welder can study, practice, and learn to weld effectively. The skills you develop in gas welding are the basis for all the other types of manual welding, such as MIG, TIG, and stick welding.

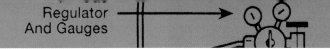

ARC WELDING (SMAW)

The arc welding process (Shielded Metal Arc Welding) is most often used for maintenance and small production welding. This process uses an electric arc generated between a flux-covered electrode and the metal being welded (base metal). Heat from the arc melts the end of the electrode and the base metal. A typical arc welding station is illustrated below.

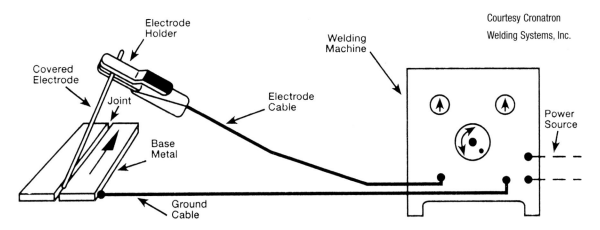

The equipment used in arc welding provides an electric current, which may either be AC (alternating current) or DC (direct current). The amount of current (amperage) is adjustable. The diameter of the electrode and thickness of the base metal will determine the kind and amount of welding current required.

Alternating Current (AC) is an electrical current which periodically reverses its direction. In a typical AC circuit, the current goes in one direction and then reverses 60 times a second, so that the current changes its direction 120 times a second.

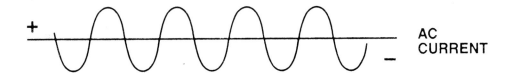

Straight Polarity (DCSP): The arc welding leads are arranged so that the electrode is the negative pole and the base metal is the positive pole. In general, DCSP will provide shallow penetration in comparison to DCRP.

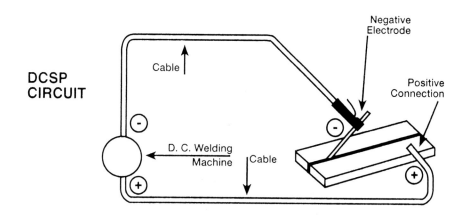

Direct Current (DC) is an electrical circuit where the electricity flows constantly and in one direction. In DC circuits electrical flow is always from the negative pole to the positive pole. In arc welding, control of the direction of electrical flow by arrangement of the poles can affect the running characteristics of an electrode and the depth of penetration.

In a DC arc welding circuit, two terms are used to define electrical flow:
DCRP–DC: Reverse polarity-Electrode positive
DCSP–DC: Straight polarity-Electrode negative

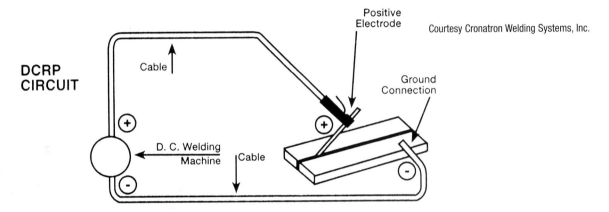

Courtesy Cronatron Welding Systems, Inc.

Reverse Polarity (DCRP): The arc welding leads are arranged so that the electrode is the positive pole and the base metal is the negative pole in the arc circuit. The decision to use DCRP depends on a number of variables including the material to be welded, the position of the weld, and the electrode being used. In general, DCRP will provide deeper penetration tha AC or DC straight polarity. DCRP yields the smoothest running characteristics.

ARC WELDING, SHIELDED METAL ARC WELDING (SMAW), STICK WELDING

Arc welding machines are available in many different sizes and capacities. The smallest arc welder illustrated in this book is a lunchbox-sized unit that plugs into 110-volt house current and will only weld thin steel and cast iron at about 60 amps. The largest arc welder illustrated in this book is a 250-amp, 220-volt unit that will weld any farm equipment on almost any farm. It will weld steel, aluminum, cast iron, and other metals. The big welders are as big as a riding lawn mower and can weigh as much as 1,000 pounds. These big welders are capable of:

- Building trailers
- Repairing broken plows
- Repairing cracks in steel frames
- Building gates, railings, and corrals
- Building trailer hitches on trucks and cars
- Burning holes in any metal except magnesium
- Cutting metal in two with a special rod
- Applying hard facing to plows and dozer blades
- Building steel frameworks for barns and sheds
- Building special farm equipment

THE ARC WELDING PROCESS

An arc welding machine rated at 250 amps can make an arc at 250 amps and 30 volts, but most farm welding is done at less than 90 to 120 amps. The stick electrode is used to make an arc on the base metal that's in the neighborhood of 10,000 degrees Fahrenheit. The electrode diameter controls the amount of heat that the welder can produce in the weld puddle. Big electrodes and high amps produce a lot of heat and penetration. Small-diameter electrodes and low amps produce small amounts of heat at the base metal. Stick-electrode welders can easily weld thin sheet metal, but the operator must be well trained. Remember that, with study and practice, you can become a good sheet-metal welder, as well.

WIRE-FEED WELDING, MIG WELDING

The name MIG denotes metal (steel or aluminum), and the word *inert* denotes a shielding gas, which is not always used. There are flux-core welding wires that do not need gas. Some of these smaller MIG welders are handy for field work where hauling a high-pressure gas bottle around would be unsafe and inconvenient. Most small MIG welders will

barely weld automotive tailpipe tubing, so be cautious about which unit you buy. A minimum-size MIG machine is shown below. Some common uses for a MIG welder are:

- Building trailers quickly
- Repairing broken farm equipment quickly
- Repairing cracks in aluminum irrigation pipe
- Repairing cracks in steel frames quickly
- Building gates, pickup racks, railings, and corrals quickly
- Building trailer hitches on trucks and cars quickly
- Building special farm equipment easily and quickly

THE MIG WELDING PROCESS

A transformer creates an electrical current somewhere between its stated/rated amperage of 90 to 400 at a current of as little as 25 to 50 volts. The wire is slowly fed out of the gun to cause a short circuit when the wire touches the metal connected by the ground clamp. A MIG welder rated at 250 amps can put out up to 250 amps at 25 volts. The resulting arc on the base metal must be shielded from atmospheric contamination, so a flux-core wire is used, or a gas such as 25 percent argon and 75 percent CO_2 is used to shield the arc. Carbon dioxide gas is used because it promotes good heat penetration, and it shields the weld from atmospheric contamination.

The number-one reason for using the wire-feed process is that it's possible to weld without stopping to pick up a stick electrode. But MIG welders have a duty cycle of as little as 30 to 60 percent. Duty cycles are rated at 10-minute intervals, and a 60-percent duty cycle means that you can weld for 6 minutes, and then you must let the welding

This 175-amp AC/DC welder can also be used as a TIG welding machine, and can be purchased for less than $1,000 secondhand. This model has been replaced by a newer 185-amp machine with more features. It weighs about 200 pounds and can do a very good job on a farm or ranch.

This MIG welder runs on 110-volt house current and plugs into a 15-amp grounded house socket. It's rated at 125 amps, but will only weld thin tailpipe material and thin aluminum. It can weld with flux-core wire or gas.

MIG WELDING

MIG (Metal Inert Gas) welding is also known as Gas Metal arc welding (GMAW). MIG is a welding process that uses an arc between a continuous filler metal electrode and the base metal. Equipment required for MIG welding is shown below:

Courtesy Cronatron Welding Systems, Inc.

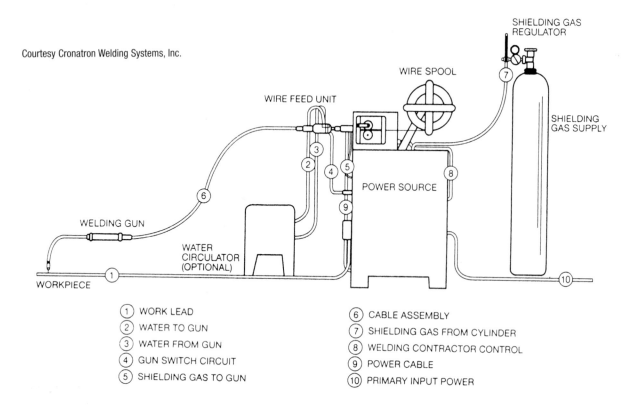

1	WORK LEAD	6	CABLE ASSEMBLY
2	WATER TO GUN	7	SHIELDING GAS FROM CYLINDER
3	WATER FROM GUN	8	WELDING CONTRACTOR CONTROL
4	GUN SWITCH CIRCUIT	9	POWER CABLE
5	SHIELDING GAS TO GUN	10	PRIMARY INPUT POWER

The basic equipment components are the welding gun and cable assembly, wire feed unit, power supply, and source of shielding gas. The gun guides the wire and conducts the electrical current and shielding gas. The shielding gas enhances weld quality and keeps impurities out of the puddle.

TYPICAL FARM WELDING PROCESSES

machine cool for 4 minutes. If you don't allow the welding machine to cool, it can overheat and burn out the transformer. MIG welders are considered to be the easiest to use of all welding machines, and they are able to weld for longer periods of time than stick welding machines. MIG welders can produce up to 10,000 degrees Fahrenheit at the puddle.

PLASMA ARC CUTTING EQUIPMENT

These miracle cutting tools are really handy if you have at least 60 pounds of air pressure and at least 110 volts of electrical power in your shop or on the farm. Cutting steel angle with an oxyacetylene cutting torch is an easy, time-proven way to cut steel quickly, but if you don't want to haul the high-pressure gas bottles around, there is a better and easier

way to cut any metal, including aluminum, stainless steel, copper, and brass. An oxyacetylene cutting torch will only cut ferrous metals except cast iron, which means it will only cut metals that are magnetic and have iron in the alloy. Nonferrous metals are not magnetic, including most of the over 100 kinds of stainless steel, aluminum, copper, and brass.

There will likely be times when you really need to cut a piece of aluminum that's too big for a tin snip or a small shear. Your oxyacetylene torch is not good for this work, but your plasma cutter will do a superb job.

Plasma cutter machines come in portable sizes that are no larger than a breadbox and weigh less than 30 pounds. Some of these machines can plug into either 110 or 220 volt circuits, and several companies make units that have a

Regulator
And Gauges

A plasma cutter like this will do many jobs that an oxyacetylene torch will not do, such as cut aluminum, copper, or brass. It runs on 110 or 220 volts and will cut through ¼-inch steel plate, as it's doing in this photo. At 220 volts, it will cut 3/8-inch steel plate. The machine only weighs 29 pounds.

You might consider setting up a hearth/forge like this one for bending steel and melting aluminum to make castings. Be safe and make the shop out of non-flammable stone or bricks. The electric blower is inside the wooden box beside the hearth. Courtesy New Mexico Farm and Ranch Museum

TYPICAL FARM WELDING PROCESSES

BROKEN BOLT REMOVAL MADE EASY

One thing that can ruin your day on the farm or ranch is a broken bolt in a piece of equipment that you need to operate before you can finish the day's work. Here's a way to fix the problem quickly.

Assuming that you have a pound or two of special Cronatron Cronaweld 333 stick electrodes in your shop, you can remove the broken stud in just a few minutes. Follow the procedure shown in the drawing:

1. Figure 1 shows a cross-section of a housing where a stud is broken off below the surface of the housing.
2. As shown in Figure 1, place the Cronaweld 333 electrode in the center of the threaded hole. Keep the electrode perpendicular and strike an arc on the center of the broken stud. Avoid tilting the electrode so as not to arc on the threads in the housing.
3. While maintaining a short arc, use a slight circular motion (not to exceed two times the diameter of the electrode) and fill the hole with weld deposit. As the electrode melts off, the flux will form a protective barrier between the weld deposit and the threads.
4. Continue the procedure to build up a column of weld metal until it reaches the surface of the housing as shown in Figure 2. Break the arc by lifting the Cronaweld 333 electrode straight up. Do not allow the weld deposit to roll over onto the housing surface.
5. Chip the slag away from the top of the weld deposit and place a washer (used for spacing) and a nut over the deposit as shown in Figure 3. The nut should be approximately equal to the diameter of the broken stud.
6. Weld the nut to the Cronaweld 333 deposit and completely fill the inside of the nut with weld metal.
7. Allow the stud, Cronaweld 333 deposit, and welded nut to completely cool to room temperature. Do not quench.
8. Using a hand wrench, remove the broken stud as shown in Figure 4.
9. After the broken stud is removed, chase the threads with the proper size tap to remove any remaining slag and clean up the threads.

For Out-of-Position (Not Vertical) Broken Studs

Use the same procedure as for flat applications with the following exceptions:

1. Amperage settings for removal of broken studs overhead might need to be reduced approximately 10 percent from the settings for flat-position applications.
2. Continuous arc and buildup may not be possible. The buildup can be obtained with short, intermittent welds. Make sure to hold the electrode vertical so as to not arc on the threads.

This procedure is courtesy of Cronatron Welding Co.

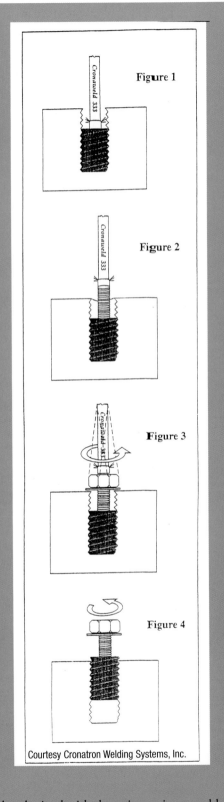

Figure 1

Figure 2

Figure 3

Figure 4

Courtesy Cronatron Welding Systems, Inc.

Regulator
And Gauges

This is stick welding (SMAW), which uses a common number of electrodes. With this type of welding there is less spatter and it looks nice when it is welded. The welding rod is number 6013. It's a good idea to do stick welding where you won't start a fire. Gayle Finch

It's relatively easy to build a new trailer to suit your needs if you have a stick welding machine. This trailer is going to be used to haul a Miller Bobcat 225-amp gasoline-powered portable welding machine. The trailer will be covered with steel sheeting to protect the welding machine and other equipment from sparks, dust, and inclement weather. Pueblo Pipe and Steel

TYPICAL FARM WELDING PROCESSES

built-in air compressor. Prices start at about $1,000 and go up from there.

THE PLASMA CUTTING PROCESS

The plasma cutting machine produces a very hot arc at about 50,000 degrees Fahrenheit, and when the trigger is pressed, an air stream of about 60 to 70 psi is blown through the torch tip, causing the extremely hot metal to be blown away, which creates a pencil-thin kerf with very little dross or slag at the cut. The cutting process is usually so efficient that a simple piece of 1x2-inch lumber can be used as a straightedge without scorching the wood.

43

This little welding machine is actually a 205-amp inverter-powered stick and TIG welder. It's completely portable at only 33 pounds total weight. In this picture, it's being operated by a 4,000-watt gasoline generator that's barely visible outside the door behind it. A generator is needed because adequate electricity isn't available.

The 205-amp stick/TIG welder in the previous picture is being operated by this 8-horsepower Briggs and Stratton generator. The welding machine worked great at an 85-amp setting, but the generator would bog down and stall at higher amp settings. A 6,000-watt generator would let the welder operate at nearly full power. The welder sells for $2,200 new.

Almost every farm welding project begins with cutting steel to the sizes listed in the project's instructional diagrams. A cheap cut-off saw like this one costs only $75 new. More expensive saws might last longer, but this one could last 10 years.

GAS WRENCH OR OXY WRENCH

Quite a few farmers and ranchers call an oxygen-acetylene cutting torch by its nicknames. No matter what you call it, the process is the same. You use a 6,200 degree Fahrenheit flame to remove rusty nuts and bolts, and to take things apart quickly. It's common to see a pair of oxyacetylene bottles in the back of a farmer's pickup truck for emergency repairs out in the field. It only takes about a minute to turn on the gas, adjust the regulators, light the torch, and have a flame that no steel can resist. The torch will not cut aluminum, stainless steel, or cast iron. Chapter 5 explains the proper procedure for using the gas cutting torch to cut steel and for emergency heating.

The basic cutting process involves using the 6,200 degree Fahrenheit heat from the torch to start a small molten puddle on the surface of the steel, and then a much higher pressure blast of oxygen will effectively oxidize the metal and blow it away, but only in the thin line under the torch. This line of severed steel is called a kerf.

One trick that you can try while using the gas cutting torch is to start the molten puddle with the oxygen and acetylene, push the trigger to start the cut, and after the cut is established and while maintaining a smooth cut movement, turn off the acetylene and watch the oxygen continue the cut for as long as you maintain a smooth cutting action. What this trick shows is that the cut is being accomplished by oxidizing the steel.

It sure makes the job go faster when all the steel tubing is cut to length, and it makes the job much like building from a kit. This pile of 1¼-inch steel tubing will soon become a pipe rack for a pickup.

A small plasma cutter is good for all metals up to ⅜-inches thick. In this picture, a piece of mild steel is being cut, but the plasma cutter also works very well on aluminum and stainless steel. Many farmers and ranchers have used the plasma cutter to cut decorative gate signs for their driveway entrances.

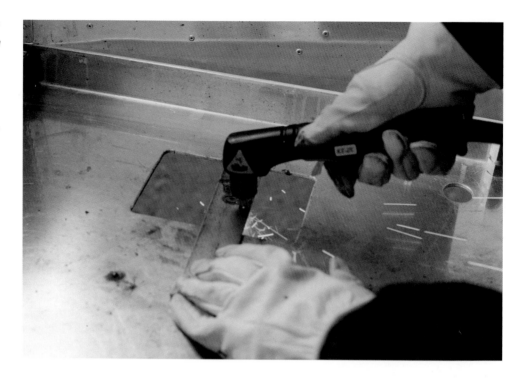

Norvall Bookout built the steel-frame pole barn on the right. He used his cousin's trailer-mounted gasoline-powered arc welder to attach the roof to the poles. The Farmall tractor in the background is still in good running condition.

CHAPTER 4
IDENTIFYING METALS IN THE FARM WELDING SHOP

WEATHER PROTECTION

It's a real problem when you go out to your stockpile of angle and sheet steel to round up enough material to build a trailer only to find that your stock is badly rusted from exposure to rain and snow. On the other hand, if you put a weather cover over the rack of steel, it can last for many years if it's kept relatively dry. Most new steel tubing comes with a good coat of oil on the inside and outside of the tubes.

Angle and channel steel ordinarily aren't coated with oil, but you can spray each length of angle and channel with a light coat of used 90-weight differential oil to preserve it and prevent rust. A permanent corrugated tin roof will protect your stock of steel in most climates, but walls will add to the weather protection, too.

BUYING STEEL AND ALUMINUM STOCK

In most areas of the country, telephone books will list "Iron and Steel" in the yellow pages. Sometimes local businesses will sell junk scrap metal rather than new, but scrap metal can be alright if it can be economically salvaged. You don't want to spend more money on the cutting torch and grinding wheels than what the new metal would cost. Many of the welded pipe fences and corrals are made from used pipe and they will last nearly a lifetime.

BUYING NEW STOCK

The best thing about buying new steel and aluminum is that you can specify the sizes you need. For instance, most pipe racks on pickup trucks are made from either 1- or 1½-inch-square steel tubing. A few pipe racks (or lumber racks) are made from 1-inch-diameter round tubing or ¾-inch inside-diameter black gas pipe, with an outside of just over 1 inch. Black gas pipe is actually very strong and will outlast many new pickup trucks.

SHEET/PLATE

It's a good idea to have a stock of aluminum step plate—also called diamond plate—with alternating raised embossing.

Use your magnetic jigging tool to check the metal to see if it's ferrous or non-ferrous. If the magnet sticks to the metal, it's ferrous, contains iron, and is either steel or cast iron. If the magnet doesn't stick, the metal is non-ferrous and may be aluminum, copper, or brass.

Make a wall rack to hold your angle steel and tubing off the floor so it won't corrode or clutter your workshop. This wall rack is made from angle shelf brackets that are screwed to the wall, and it holds thin-wall 4130 chrome-moly aircraft tubing.

This section of irrigation tubing contains both aluminum and steel, but the aluminum pipe looks rusty from shallow well water containing a lot of minerals and iron. A magnet test of this pipe assembly would show which parts are steel and which are aluminum.

The sheet metal, made from either aluminum or steel, can be purchased in 4x8-foot rectangular sheets. A plasma cutter can quickly cut the large sheet into smaller pieces for projects. Stainless steel is fun to cut with a plasma cutter. An oxyacetylene cutting torch will do a great job of cutting any sheet metal from car fender material up to the thickest steel you can handle. So it's better to buy 4x8-foot sheets of everything from aluminum to stainless steel to mild steel sheet, because it's much more economical to buy full sheets.

ANGLE STEEL

With angle steel (an older term is angle iron), get an assortment of leg widths from 1 to 3 inches for your stock rack. The thicker web sections will be good for building strong structures, and the thinner, lighter web sections will be suitable for more delicate structures. Angle steel usually comes in 20-foot lengths, but you can also find good deals on remnants. Some steel suppliers will sell this material by the pound or stick rather than by the foot.

This irrigation piping and wheels contains two kinds of metals. The pipe is aluminum, and the wheels are made from steel. The spokes of the wheels are steel, too. This requires different welding rods and equipment. See Chapters 6 and 9 for the proper welding methods.

STORAGE RACKS

Whether you have 5 sticks or 50 sticks of tubing, you don't want it to be laying around on the floor where you could trip on it. The best way to store tubing and angle pipe is on a rack with 8-inch-long pegs on a vertical pole. About 4 poles will support a 20-foot stick of pipe and angle. Sheets of metal are also a nuisance if they're left lying on the floor, plus they'll corrode if you store them on damp concrete. A good storage rack for 4x8-foot sheets of metal is an A-frame rack on wheels that the sheets can lean on from either side. Just make sure that the sheet metal isn't too heavy for your rack and that your rack is strong enough to support your sheets.

IDENTIFYING METALS

After you spend a lot of time welding and working with metal, you'll become accustomed to identifying metals by looking at them, but to be sure, you can always use a magnet to determine if a metal is ferrous or nonferrous. Ferrous metals contain iron, which is magnetic. Nonferrous metals, such as aluminum, brass, and copper, have no iron and are not magnetic. If you're unsure if your metal is ferrous, use one of your jigging magnets to find out. But note the difference in working with stainless steel: there are over 100 different alloys of stainless steel—such as numbers 304, 308, and 316—and most stainless steels are nonmagnetic even though they are ferrous metals. A magnet will not be attracted to stainless steel. Sometimes rusty water will stain the metal so it looks like rusty steel, but in reality the metal may really be stained aluminum or stainless steel. Note the two charts in this chapter that show you how to use the grinder test to determine which type of metal you're working with. Be aware that aluminum will not create sparks, and it will clog up a grinding wheel. Stainless steel will create sparks when it's ground with an abrasive wheel.

PREPARATION OF METAL FOR WELDING

In every instance prior to welding, the metal should be clean, free of rust and corrosion, and free of paint. Sanding all metals with an abrasive 80-grit flap wheel will assist in making a good weld. Steel and iron can also be treated with metal prep (phosphoric acid) and rinsed in clean water to make a better weld. Aluminum can be cleaned for welding by using a commercial aluminum prep that contains phosphoric acid. Be sure to rinse the aluminum with clear water after it's been etched. If aluminum isn't thoroughly clean it cannot be effectively welded. The welding or brazing rod will just roll off the metal without fusing or sticking. That will be your clue that you haven't properly cleaned the metal.

ROD FOR DIRTY METAL

You will find that some welding rods are advertised to weld through rust, oil, or paint, and that is true. One example is Cronatron 321, a 70,000-psi tensile-strength rod. Another common arc welding rod for rusty, dirty steel is AWS 6011, a 60,000-psi tensile-strength rod. The rod for mild steel angle, channel, and plate is rated at 60,000-psi tensile strength. That means that a 1-inch-square bar of mild steel 1 inch square, could support about 60,000 pounds in a pull test. See Chapter 10 for more about the strengths of welding rod.

METAL IDENTIFICATION CHART

Courtesy Cronatron Welding Systems, Inc.

TEST	Manganese Steel	Stainless Steel	Low Carbon Steel mild steel .30% carbon & below	Medium Carbon Steel .30 to .45% carbon
Appearance	Dull cast finish	Bright, smooth surface lines	Gray fine	Gray finish
Fracture	Rough grained	Bright appearance	Gray bright crystalline	Light gray
Magnetic	Non-magnetic	Depends on exact composition	Highly magnetic	Highly magnetic
Torch	Turns bright red & melts quickly	Turns bright red & melts quickly	Gives off sparks when melted & pool solidifies rapidly	Melts quickly & gives off some sparks
Chip	Hard to chip	Smooth chip, smooth bright color	Chips easily smooth, long chip	Chips easily smooth, long chip
Spark	Bright white bursts · heavy pattern	Very few short full red sparks with few forks	Long white sparks some forks near end of stream	Long white sparks with secondary bursts along stream
Volume of stream	Moderately large	Moderate	Moderately large	Moderately large
Spark Configuration				

METAL IDENTIFICATION CHART

Courtesy Cronatron Welding Systems, Inc.

TEST	High Carbon Steel 45% carbon & above	Wrought Iron	Cast Iron	High Sulfur Steel
Appearance	Dark gray smooth finish	Gray, fine surface lines	Rough, very dull gray	Dark Gray
Fracture	Light grayish white, and finer grained than low carbon steel	Fibrous structure, split in the direction which the fibers run	Brittle gray	Gray, very fine grain
Magnetic	Highly magnetic	Highly magnetic	Highly magnetic	Highly magnetic
Torch	Melts quickly & molten metal is brighter than low carbon steel	Melts quickly & has a slight tendency to spark	Turns dull red first, puddle is very fluid, no sparks	Melts quickly turns bright red before melting
Chip	Difficult to chip because of brittleness	Chips easily continuous chip	Very small brittle chips	Chips easily, smooth, long chip
Spark	Large volume of brilliant white sparks	Straw colored sparks near wheel, few white forks near the end of the stream	Dull red sparks formed close to the wheel	Bright carrier lines with cigar shaped swells
Volume of stream	Moderate	Large	Small	Large
Spark Configuration				

CHAPTER 5
OXYACETYLENE CUTTING, HEATING, AND PLASMA CUTTING

Angle, sheet, channel, and bar steels will bend like warm taffy when heated to about dark red, or 1,250 degrees Fahrenheit. It will really move around when it's heated to medium red, or 2,100 degrees Fahrenheit. It will also change its molecular structure if it's held at that temperature for several hours. It will start to scale, flake off, and become weak and brittle because of molecular changes in its structure. Refer to the Tempil chart (opposite page) to see what happens when you heat steel—temperature really makes a difference because steel is sensitive to heating and cooling cycles.

However, the bending and softening characteristics of heated steel products can be quite helpful when you make repairs and build equipment for farming and ranching operations. A piece of ¾-inch black gas pipe that will collapse when it's bent cold, will bend quite nicely when heated to

These sticks of small-diameter steel rods have been heated to medium red and held at that temperature for several minutes. They are flaking and scaling so much that the red heat of the steel is hardly visible. Steel can become soft or brittle if it's held at the temperature too long. Courtesy New Mexico Farm and Ranch Heritage Museum

Basic Guide to Ferrous Metallurgy

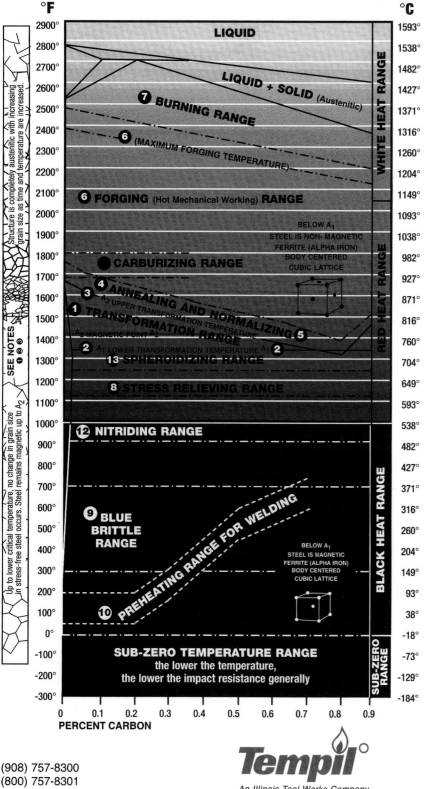

1 TRANSFORMATION RANGE- In this range steels undergo internal atomic changes which radically affect the properties of the material.

2 LOWER TRANSFORMATION TEMPERATURE (A_1). Termed Ac_1 on heating, Ar_1 on cooling. Below Ac_1 structure ordinarily consists of FERRITE and PEARLITE (see below). On heating through Ac_1 these constituents begin to dissolve in each other to form AUSTENITE (see below) which is non-magnetic. This dissolving action continues on heating through the TRANSFORMATION RANGE until the solid solution is complete at the upper transformation temperature.

3 UPPER TRANSFORMATION TEMPERATURE (A_3). Termed Ac_3 on heating, Ar_3 on cooling. Above this temperature the structure consists wholly of AUSTENITE which coarsens with increasing time and temperature. Upper transformation temperature is lowered as carbon increases to 0.85% (eutectoid point).

● FERRITE is practically pure iron (in plain carbon steels) existing below the lower transformation temperature. It is magnetic and has very slight solid solubility for carbon.

● PEARLITE is a mechanical mixture of FERRITE and CEMENTITE.

● CEMENTITE or IRON CARBIDE is a compound of iron and carbide, Fe_3C.

● AUSTENITE is the non-magnetic form of iron and has the power to dissolve carbon and alloying elements.

4 ANNEALING, frequently referred to as FULL ANNEALING, consists of heating steels to slightly above Ac_3, holding for AUSTENITE to form, then slowly cooling in order to produce small grain size, softness, good ductility and other desirable properties. On cooling slowly the AUSTENITE transforms to FERRITE and PEARLITE.

5 NORMALIZING consists of heating steels to slightly above Ac_3, holding for AUSTENITE to form, then followed by cooling (in still air). On cooling, AUSTENITE transforms giving somewhat higher strength and hardness and slightly less ductility than in annealing.

6 FORGING RANGE extends to several hundred degrees above the UPPER TRANSFORMATION TEMPERATURE.

7 BURNING RANGE is above the FORGING RANGE. Burned steel is ruined and *cannot be cured* except by remelting.

8 STRESS RELIEVING consists of heating to a point below the LOWER TRANSFORMATION TEMPERATURE, A_1, holding for a sufficiently long period to relieve locked-up stresses, then slowly cooling. This process is sometimes called PROCESS ANNEALING.

9 BLUE BRITTLE RANGE occurs approximately from 300° to 700°F. Peening or working of steels should not be done between these temperatures, since they are more brittle in this range than above or below it.

10 PREHEATING FOR WELDING is carried out to prevent crack formation. See TEMPIL® PREHEATING CHART for recommended temperature for various steels and non-ferrous metals.

11 CARBURIZING consists of dissolving carbon into surface of steel by heating to above transformation range in presence of carburizing compounds.

12 NITRIDING consists of heating certain *special steels* to about 1000°F for long periods in the presence of ammonia gas. Nitrogen is absorbed into the surface to produce extremely hard "skins".

13 SPHEROIDIZING consists of heating to just below the lower transformation temperature, A_1, for a sufficient length of time to put the CEMENTITE constituent of PEARLITE into popular form. This produces softness and in many cases good machinability.

● MARTENSITE is the hardest of the transformation products of AUSTENITE and is formed only on cooling below a certain temperature known as the M_s temperature (about 400° to 600°F for carbon steels). Cooling to this temperature must be sufficiently rapid to prevent AUSTENITE from transforming to softer constituents at higher temperatures.

● EUTECTOID STEEL contains approximately 0.85% carbon.

● FLAKING occurs in many alloy steels and is a defect characterized by localized micro-cracking and "flake-like" fracturing. It is usually attributed to hydrogen bursts. Cure consists of cooling to at least 600°F before air-cooling.

● OPEN OR RIMMING STEEL has not been completely deoxidized and the ingot solidifies with a sound surface ("rim") and a core portion containing blowholes which are welded in subsequent hot rolling.

● KILLED STEEL has been deoxidized at least sufficiently to solidify without appreciable gas evolution.

● SEMI-KILLED STEEL has been partially deoxidized to reduce solidification shrinkage in the ingot.

● A SIMPLE RULE: Brinell Hardness divided by two, times 1000, equals approximate Tensile Strength in pounds per square inch. (200 Brinell ÷ 2 x 1000 = approx. 100,000 Tensile Strength, p.s.i.).

(908) 757-8300
(800) 757-8301

An Illinois Tool Works Company

www.tempil.com

WELDING ON THE DISTAFF SIDE

Leslie Abercrombie is a 20-year-old college student who lives on her family farm near Tularosa, New Mexico, and she is an accomplished welder. Leslie has lived in this part of south-central New Mexico all her life. She attended high school in Alamogordo and first became interested in welding while taking an ag-mechanics class. She took a more advanced class in welding, and as a member of FFA, she entered an FFA welding contest at the Otero County Fair. She won the reserve grand championship with a farm-gate sign-welding project. She beat out all the boys except one!

Leslie's family owns a medium-sized farm north of Tularosa, where they raise cows and goats. Like many farm families, her parents also work in town at other jobs. Her mom is a guidance counselor, and her dad works as a soil conservation agent in Otero County. Leslie attends New Mexico State University in Las Cruces. During her first summer after she graduated from high school, Leslie participated in the state division of the Miss America Pageant and was chosen as Miss Otero County.

Leslie has used her welding talents to help pay for college. She spent the summer as a welder, fitter, and ranch hand at the Mesa Verde Ranch in New Mexico. She fitted and welded pipe corrals along with other ranch-hand chores. She commutes over 80 miles each way to attend college. During her sophomore year, she started working part-time in the endocrinology lab on campus doing genotyping experiments. Leslie has declared a double major in animal science and history, and is working toward a Ph.D. so she can become a college professor.

—Gayle Finch

Leslie Abercrombie adjusts a Harris cutting torch to make the rich acetylene flame turn into a neutral, equal-gas cutting flame. Here you see a lot of smoke and soot from the flame.

medium to bright red. The yellow range of heating steel is considered to be the burning range, after which the steel is ruined and can't be fixed except by remelting.

For the home and farm shop, it's very important to do the heating and then avoid holding the heat in the steel for long periods of time, which could be for only several minutes, especially if the hot steel is exposed to wind drafts. Mild steel pipe, angle, and plate is less susceptible to this damage than is chrome-moly (4130) steel. The important thing is to not be bashful or timid with heating and welding steel or any other farm metal. Heat it and then get out of there and let it cool.

CUTTING TORCH OPERATION

In order to cleanly cut steel, first open the oxygen tank valve all the way so the valve seals won't let the high-pressure 2,250-psi gas leak out. This valve must always be either fully on or fully off to prevent leaking.

Next, open the acetylene tank valve about ¾ths of a turn. This is because the tank only holds 250 psi, about ⅒th as

OXY-ACETYLENE CUTTING AND HEATING TORCH TIPS

Cutting torch tips are relatively inexpensive. Stock up on several sizes, and the sizes depend on the thicknesses you will need to cut and heat. Here are some suggestions for tips to stock:

Size No. 000: Use for sheet steel up to ³⁄₁₆-inch thick. Use oxygen pressures of 15 to 30 psi.

Size No. 00: Use for steel from ³⁄₁₆-inch up to ³⁄₈-inch thick. Use oxygen pressures of 20 to 30 psi.

Size No. 0: Use for steel from ³⁄₈-inch up to ⅝-inch thick. Use oxygen pressures of 30 to 40 psi.

Size No. 1: Use for steel plate of ⅝-inch up to 1-inch thick. Use oxygen pressures of 35 to 50 psi.

Size No. 2: Use for steel plate of 1-inch up to 2-inch thick. Use oxygen pressures of 40 to 55 psi.

Size No. 3: Use for steel plate of 2-inch up to 3-inch thick . Use oxygen pressures of 45 to 60 psi.

Examples: When cutting and fishmouthing 2 inch, No. 40 schedule steel pipe, which has a wall thickness of ¼ inch, use a No. 00 cutting tip. Don't think about the outside diameter of the pipe, which is somewhat over 2½ inches, but think about the actual wall thickness of the pipe. When cutting through a 55 gallon oil drum, use the smallest cutting tip, which is a No. 000, normally used for cutting sheet metal. If you own a plasma cutter, this isthe best way to cut a drum. If you are cutting with a torch, make the initial cut and lay the torch as flat to the metal as possible to prevent getting a rough, slag edge. Practice on some sheet metal before starting to cut through the steel drum.

CAUTION! Do not try to cut even one single small hole in a closed drum unless it has been purged or filled with water. Even 55 gallon wax drums have been known to explode and kill the welder because of the wax vapors in the drum. These vapors are as explosive as gasoline in the right conditions. Remember that even wheat dust can explode in certain conditions. In Abilene, Texas, in the 1960s, a welder was blown over 50 feet into the air and through the welding shop roof when he first pierced a 55 gallon drum that had been used for floor wax. Don't take any chances with your life by cutting any closed vessel without purging it or filling it with water first.

HOW A CUTTING TORCH WORKS

Before you light the torch, turn it up toward you and look at the business end of the tip. You will see six small holes around the outside of the flat part of the tip. These six holes are the pre-heat holes. These holes are similar to the single hole in a gas welding tip. They act to light and adjust the flame, just like the tip of a similar sized welding tip. When you light the torch and adjust it for a neutral flame, the six flames act to provide heat to the steel part that you intend to cut. These six flames have no part in actually severing steel. The center, larger oxygen-only hole is the one that makes the cut.

The one center hole is usually about twice the size as one of the pre-heat holes. If you open the oxygen valve on the handle to full open and adjust the oxygen regulator to the psi recommended in the chart above, you will be able to press the trigger and get a strong flow of oxygen out of the center hole, but you will not get any flame out of the hole at any time during the cutting process. This center hole is the one that actually makes the cut in steel after the steel is red hot and is starting to melt or puddle. The oxygen coming out of the center hole actually oxidizes the steel and blows it away to make the cut.

To prove to yourself that the center hole is the only hole that makes the cut in steel, try starting the cut and then shut off the acetylene at the torch and continue the cut without any flame at all. Try it and you will like it. Then you can impress all your farm and ranch friends with your special skills as a welder.

A factory-made dolly cart is used here to hold a set of oxyacetylene tanks that are attached to a Smiths torch with a cutting attachment. The small acetylene tank is a 60-cubic-foot size, and the larger oxygen tank is a 125-cubic-foot size, which is useful if you're doing a lot of cutting work.

This small, portable oxyacetylene welding set only holds 20 cubic feet of oxygen and 10 cubic feet of acetylene, but in a pinch you can easily lift the whole set and put it in the back of your pickup or in the open (not closed) trunk of your car. The whole setup costs $280 at a discount store plus $10 each to fill the tanks with gas.

much pressure as the oxygen tank. Also, if you accidentally have a backfire that burns inside the hose and torch, it will be faster to shut off the acetylene if the valve is only turned ¾ of the way on. The acetylene won't leak when it's only partially turned on.

Set the oxygen regulator to 20 psi for steel under ⅜-inch thick.

Set the acetylene regulator to 5 to 6 psi for steel under ⅜-inch thick.

Open the oxygen valve on the torch body to the fully on position. This is where you get the high pressure you need to cut when you hit the trigger.

With the spark striker in your left hand (if you are right-handed), open the acetylene valve to about ¾ths turn, but no more than that. Quickly—before you stink up the shop with acetylene gas—strike the spark and light the torch. The

This oxygen regulator and gauges are taken apart to show you that there is very little gas volume inside the regulating chamber. The wing screw to the right is screwed against the cup and spring, which pushes against the rubber diaphragm, which in turn pushes in the valve in the middle of the regulator body to keep the pressure at a set amount.

Another view of the oxygen regulator shows a different side of the rubber diaphragm that pushes against the valve in the center of the regulator to hold a set pressure. There is really nothing to cause a fire unless the regulator is modified or tampered with.

resulting flame will be red and very smoky. If the red flame is jumping away from the torch tip, close the acetylene valve slightly until the flame comes back to the torch tip.

So you don't smoke up the shop with the carbon that comes off the acetylene flame, quickly open the cutting torch oxygen valve to make a neutral flame. The flame should now look like the flame in the drawing in Chapter 3.

When the flame is properly adjusted to neutral, pull the trigger all the way back, and the flame will get much louder, the acetylene will draw back toward the tip, and the oxygen will make a much louder sound. When you can do this, you are ready to cut steel.

A good rule of thumb is to hold the flame close to the steel, count to 10, and if you have a small, shiny red puddle on the

As Leslie adds more oxygen, the smoke starts to dissipate, but the flame still needs more oxygen. Equal parts of oxygen and acetylene are used in cutting, just as in welding.

part you want to cut, then you are ready to press the oxygen trigger. The steel will be blown out of a kerf where the flame is. Then slowly, about 1 inch every 5 seconds, move the torch and cut a kerf in the steel.

If you can't make a shiny red puddle in the count of 10, you need a larger tip on the cutting torch.

Shutting Off the Cutting Torch

When the cut is done, turn off the oxygen valve first, then shut off the acetylene valve last. If you don't shut down in that order, you will get a very loud pop from the torch. This resulting loud popping sound could possibly cause a torch flash-back, and it will soot up the torch every time.

Leslie is bracing her right hand with her left hand to ensure a smooth cut line. She's also bracing her arm on the bench vise for greater steadiness. The expanded metal in the top of the welding and cutting table makes a good place to cut metal without sparks flying everywhere.

Then, when you're done cutting for the day, shut off the oxygen tank and the acetylene tank. Some companies continue to suggest that you should bleed off each regulator to zero, but if you count the cubic feet of acetylene you will bleed off into the atmosphere during your lifetime, you may not want to do it that way. The "bleed-off each time" theory is that if you have oil, grease, trash, and a ruptured regulator diaphragm, it "might" cause a fire in your regulator. But if you have oil, grease, trash, and a ruptured regulator, you shouldn't be using them in the first place. Replace dirty and damaged regulators *before* you use them.

Leslie displays a farm gate metal sculpture that she made while she was a member of the FFA in high school. The images were cut from a steel plate with a cutting torch and then welded to the frame with an arc welding machine. The sculpture will be placed at the gate to the farm.

MORE CUTTING AND HEATING TIPS

If you have a lot of cutting to do, such as disassembling a piece of old equipment for scrap, you can save a little money by using MAPP gas (a combination of liquefied petroleum and methacetylene-propadiene) in place of acetylene. You can also use propane to substitute for acetylene. Propane is even cheaper than MAPP gas.

In one example, a large welding training facility in the South always bleeds off the regulators at the end of each day, and the upstairs offices always stink of acetylene, which creates a potentially explosive atmosphere in both the offices and in the welding classroom. It could be that the welding gas industry knows they will sell more gas if you bleed off the regulators each day. One positive thing about not bleeding off the regulators is that if you still find yesterday's pressure showing on the gauges, you know that your regulators and torch and hoses don't have any leaks!

Troubleshooting Your Cutting Torch Expertise

- If the torch pops loudly but doesn't light when you try to light it, you don't have enough acetylene pressure or flow. Open the acetylene valve on the torch body another ¼ turn and try again.
- For most steel cutting, regardless of the steel thickness, don't use more than 5 or 6 psi of acetylene.
- If you don't have a shiny molten puddle on the steel by the count of 10 when trying your cut, then turn up the heat by increasing the torch valve openings. If you still don't have enough heat, then go to a larger number tip.
- If you're piercing some holes, expect the tip to get dirty pretty fast. Check the tip and clean it often.
- The thickness of the steel determines the amount of oxygen needed to make the cut. Turn up the oxygen pressure if the cut is slower than normal, or go to a larger-number tip.
- For ¼-inch-thick steel, use 20 to 30 psi oxygen pressure. Check the chart on page 55.
- For 1-inch-thick steel, use 35 to 50 psi oxygen pressure and 5 psi acetylene pressure.

TROUBLESHOOTING YOUR CUTTING TORCH PROBLEMS

The most common problem that welders encounter when first learning how to cut steel is that the cut will bubble and not cut all the way through the steel. The cut looks really bad and the parts will not come apart. This is caused by not enough oxygen pressure. Look at the chart on page 55 and adjust your gauges accordingly.

The second most common problem with oxygen-acetylene cutting is that the cut is not where you wanted it to be. This is often caused by trying to cut thinner steel with a tip that is too big. In this instance, the pre-heat flames are melting the metal around the cut. These flames are only for pre-heating and not for the cutting process. Again, look at the chart for a suitable sized cutting tip.

Another common problem of even experienced welders is having only one size cutting tip. This tip is used for everything, which is just like using one hammer to build an entire barn. Use the correct size cutting tip for each metal thickness you cut.

When sparks blow back at you and no cut is made, you are probably using too small of a tip, but more likely you do not have enough oxygen pressure and may not have preheated the steel to its melting point. You must have a melted spot on the steel, even if it is just a tiny melted spot, before you press the oxygen trigger to start the cut. Also if you press the oxygen trigger too soon before you have a melted spot, the resulting oxygen flow will actually cool the metal and no cut will happen, no matter how long you hold the trigger down.

If your cut looks pretty good, but you have a lot of slag hanging down on the bottom of the cut, you have been moving the torch too slow. Move a little faster and see if the slag will go away on the rest of your cut. For cuts that have already been done, you can clean up the back side slag with a 4-inch angle grinder.

Like all things in life, practice is the way to improve your techniques. Practice, practice, practice.

ACETYLENE PRESSURES

Notice that the acetylene low-pressure gauge is red at and above 15 psi. That's because acetylene becomes unstable and can explode at pressures above 15 psi. Also, acetylene tanks cannot have their volume depleted by more than ⅐th per hour or else they will become unstable and could explode. They cannot be filled at more than ⅐th of their volume per hour for the same reasons. Therefore, it should take at least 7 hours to refill your tank.

- Remember that aluminum and stainless steel will not oxidize, and cast iron will not easily oxidize, so don't try to cut these metals with an oxyacetylene cutting torch. Use a plasma cutting machine for cutting these metals.

Cutting torches can be used to apply heat for bending smaller, thinner pieces of steel and for applying more heat than a regular gas welding torch will produce. A cutting torch will produce about 10 times more heat than a large number-5 welding tip. But a rosebud tip will produce about 10 times more heat than a cutting torch.

NOTES ON CUTTING TORCH HANDLES AND TORCHES

Most farm equipment cutting torches are simply add-ons to a standard gas welding torch. This is a handy way to have both a welding torch and a cutting torch in one unit. You just unscrew the one tip and screw on the other tip when you want to cut or weld. Most gas welding outfits have about 90 percent use of the welding tip, and only 10 percent use of the cutting tip.

Be aware that some larger cutting torches are single purpose tips and these larger cutting torches can not be used as welding torches. The whole torch must be exchanged for a smaller or purpose-built welding tip. Even the larger tips light up and work about the same as a smaller tip. The main thing is the amount of acetylene required to light up and start the cutting flame. If your cutting torch pops and bangs when you try to light it, you probably do not have enough gas pressure or flow. Raise the pressure and try it again. If you still need more pressure to light a very large torch, then you can gang up two or more acetylene tanks for more gas volume at the torch.

The air-pressure gauge is located on the rear of the Lincoln Electric Plasma 25 cutter machine. You can also see the two air filters. One is a disposable plastic unit and the other is a permanent unit that can be cleaned. Both are needed to keep the air clean.

This automobile air-conditioner compressor bracket was modified by cutting it to fit a Corvair engine. Note the small amount of slag that will be easy to remove by grinding it with a 4-inch angle grinder. Gayle Finch

The Lincoln Electric Pro-Cut 25 is plugged into a 110-volt, 15-amp wall plug, and it is still cutting this ¼-inch steel plate easily. If it were plugged into a 220-volt, 30-amp circuit, it could easily cut ⅜-inch steel or aluminum plate. Gayle Finch

ROSEBUD TIPS

These special tips are called rosebuds because the flame they produce is very large compared to a cutting-torch tip. Most welding kits don't come with a rosebud tip, so you have to go to your local welding supply store and purchase one that fits your torch. It's a good idea to take your torch body with you when you go shopping for a rosebud tip. Also be aware that some torches cannot be fit with rosebud tips. You might need to buy a larger torch body in order to find the appropriate rosebud tip. Rosebud tips are usually used to preheat large pieces of cracked cast-iron equipment for brazing, or to preheat a steel structure for arc welding repair. Rosebud tips put out a lot of heat!

Operating a Rosebud Tip

Lighting up a rosebud takes even more acetylene flow than a cutting torch. You may need to open the torch body valves at least a full turn to light them. First-time users usually get a very loud pop on their first light-up. If you do, you need more flow, not more pressure.

Heating with a rosebud is as easy as it looks. Just hold the torch where you want the heat to be and use a Tempil stick to determine the temperature of the metal. Tempil sticks come in 2-degree Fahrenheit increments so you can be super accurate with your heating. Tempil sticks are available at your local welding supplier.

PLASMA CUTTING

Just when welders thought they had all the equipment figured out, welding equipment engineers came up with something new—the plasma cutter. At first, plasma cutting machines were as large as kitchen stoves, but now they're as small as a breadbox. Perhaps they'll be even smaller in a few years. One of the really good things that a plasma cutter can do is cut nonferrous metals. In fact, a plasma cutter will cut any metal that will conduct electricity, which includes most metals.

Say that you need a couple of pieces of stainless steel from a large sheet that you have in stock. Stainless steel will dull a hacksaw in about 10 strokes of the saw, but a plasma cutter will cut stainless steel just as fast as it will cut mild-steel sheet.

Plasma cutters can also pierce thick metal, but for a cleaner cut, first drill a small 1/8-inch hole to start the cut. Gayle Finch

Do you need to cut a straight line on a piece of 0.050-inch-thick aluminum? Here we are using a 1x2-inch board to guide the plasma torch. Note that the cut is straight and the board's straight edge is not being burned or scorched by the torch. Gayle Finch

It only took about 2 minutes to make the cut in this piece of 0.050-inch aluminum with the Lincoln plasma torch running on a 110-volt circuit. The small amount of slag or dross on the back of the cut can be easily removed with an 80-grit angle grinder, making it almost as smooth as a 4-foot shear would cut.

Aluminum can actually be cut with a carbide-tipped skill-saw blade, but cutting it with a skill-saw blade can also catch and make a jagged cut in the aluminum sheet. Thicker aluminum, 1 inch and thicker, is usually cut with a skill saw. You might want to try a skill saw on thicker pieces of aluminum, but a hacksaw would take you all day, and you'd go through a dozen new blades just to cut the thick plate.

PLASMA CUTTING OPERATION

For relatively thin metals, all you need for cutting is 110 volts, and for heavier metals 220 volts will suffice. You'll need an air compressor that's big enough to support a small spray-paint gun at about 60 to 70 psi. It's a good idea to have good oil and water filters to keep the cutting air clean. Some brands of plasma cutters have their own built-in air compressor so you don't need a separate compressor.

In most cases, a plasma cutter will cut through paint and rust. But if the torch won't start the cut, then clean off a section of the metal first. The torch should then be able to make the cut. The same trick works for oil and grease. If there's dirt on the metal, try cleaning a small place off first. Plasma cutters are great for body and fender work, and they work well for farm equipment modifications that are too small for oxyacetylene torches.

Troubleshooting the Plasma Cutter

- The most common reason for not starting or failing to continue a cut is a loose consumable. Copper orifices are considered consumables because they wear out with normal use. Check to see that the consumable is tight enough, and use a wrench if it needs to be tightened.
- If you can't cut metal, check to see if there is oil or water in the line or the torch. You shouldn't have any trouble with water or oil if you make sure that there's a good water and oil separator in the air line.

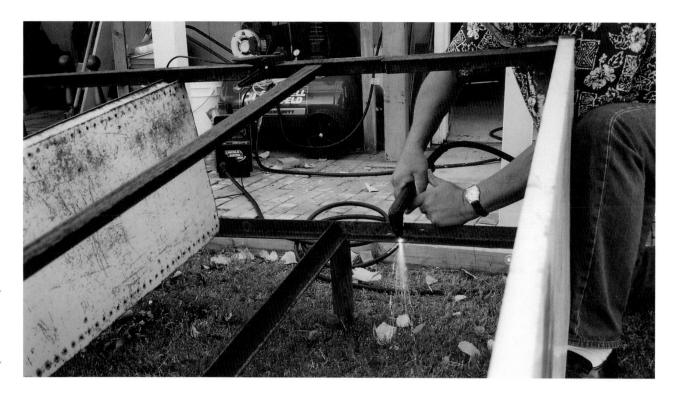

Cutting the top off a set of steel shelves is a cinch with a plug-in plasma cutter. It even cut through a significant amount of rust, as shown here. Gayle Finch

Making a vertical cut on the rusty shelving frame is easy with a plasma cutter. Note that no gloves are needed and the sparks are much smaller than with an oxyacetylene torch. Gayle Finch

It only took about four minutes to cut the four angle steel posts on this shelving. The plasma torch is still able to blow its 50,000-degree Fahrenheit flame when not cutting anything. The light from the flame isn't nearly as bright as the light from an arc welder. Gayle Finch

The Lincoln Pro-Cut 25 plasma cutting machine is also good for fish-mouth fitting tubing, including tailpipe tubing, as shown here. After the cut is made, a die grinder removes the slag from the cut line. Gayle Finch

A Miller plasma cutter is being operated by a gasoline generator and an air compressor to make a repair on this hay baler. When the broken part is removed, a replacement will be welded on by a Miller wire-feed machine. Miller Electric Company, Inc.

This plastic box contains the consumables for the Lincoln Pro-Cut 25 plasma cutting torch. The consumables are made out of copper, which resists sticking to almost all other metals. The parts should be replaced whenever they get too worn out to work properly.

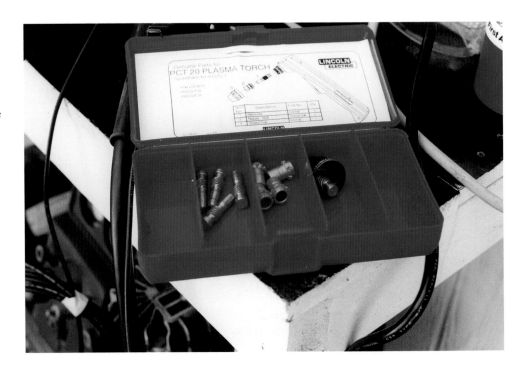

CHAPTER 6
OXYACETYLENE WELDING: STEEL, ALUMINIUM AND STAINLESS

A good-quality oxyacetylene welding rig is an absolute necessity for any farm and ranch welding shop. See Chapter 10 for a suggestion of a good, inexpensive, and portable gas-welding rig. The gas welder is very handy for soldering, brazing, fusion welding, heating, and cutting steel for your projects. Most good gas welding rigs cost under $500 for the complete setup. A turn-key rig will cost about $800, and includes a cart and extra welding and heating tips. We'll now cover what a gas welding rig can do in your shop, starting with soldering.

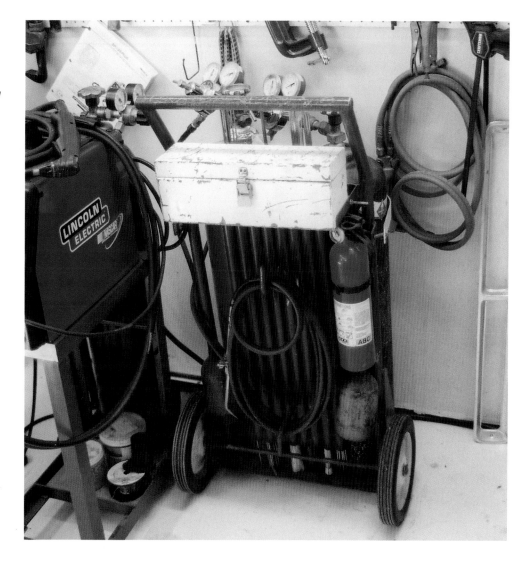

This welding cart has several tubes on the back for storing various sizes of 36-inch-long sticks of gas welding rod. The tanks (cylinders, bottles) are both 125 cubic feet. The torch is a Harris model number 15-3 aircraft welder with numbers 1, 2, and 3 size tips. This setup weighs about 200 pounds and costs about $500.

There are three types of flames used when gas welding or brazing. They are neutral, carburizing, and oxidizing.

Courtesy Cronatron Welding Co.

Neutral Flame

A neutral flame has an equal mixture of oxygen and acetylene and is normally used when you need to build up an area or when you do not want the filler metal to free flow. This is the flame used in most welding processes. A neutral flame burns at approximately 6,000 degrees Fahrenheit, which provides enough heat for fusion welding of steel and cast iron. A neutral flame can be identified by its singular inner cone which is rounded at the tip and has a bluish white color.

Carburizing Flame

A carburizing flame has a slight excess of acetylene and is normally used when you want the filler metal to be very free flowing and wet rapidly as when hardfacing and welding light metal. A carburizing flame can be identified by the size of the inner cone. The length of the inner cone is controlled by the amount of acetylene. As the acetylene is increased, the cone gets longer. The size of this cone is sometimes referred to as 2x, 3x, 4x, and so on. This refers to the length of the cone compared to the neutral flame.

Oxidizing Flame

An oxidizing flame has a slight excess of oxygen and will tend to burn the metal being welded. It is almost never used when brazing. An oxidizing flame results in a short, noisy hissing sound. The inner cone has a sharp point and is outlined in an iridescent blue color.

SOLDERING WITH GAS

Lead soldering temperature starts at 250 degrees Fahrenheit and goes up to 800 degrees Fahrenheit. Keep those temperatures in mind. Many metals can be soldered if the correct flux is used, and this includes dissimilar metals like aluminum, copper, and brass. These metals can all be soldered in various combinations with one another.

The most difficult metal to solder is mild steel. Solder doesn't stick to it at all. The easiest metals to solder are copper and stainless steel. With most kinds of solder, a flux should be used to clean the metal so the solder will stick. Most solders are available with a flux core to make cleaning automatic while soldering. Most soldering is best done with a soldering iron, which is usually electric, but if you can keep the flame from touching the flux, then torch soldering is OK. Avoid resoldering a gasoline tank with flame soldering because of the chance of fumes and explosions. A torch flame can be used to heat a metal soldering iron. Copper tubing

Continued on page 74

HOW TO DECIDE WHEN TO GAS WELD PARTS

A good rule of thumb is to gas weld when the parts to be welded are less than ⅛-inch thick and there is not a problem with excess heat. "Excessive heat" means that you should not gas weld something when the heat from the flame would be a problem, such as near a gas tank or near a painted surface where the flame could ignite.

It is entirely possible to weld a complete project with gas welding. One thing that can be gas welded is a cart for your welding tanks. This would be a good practice project to improve your welding skills. The kids on the farm would enjoy gas welding a go-kart. Of course, a good MIG welder would be faster than gas welding.

In this book, a four-wheel-drive off-road vehicle is welded with a stick welder. This was because a flame from a torch would have burned too much paint and could have started the padded seat on fire. There will also be times when the flame of the torch would not matter, such as when welding a new muffle to an exhaust pipe.

There will also be times when the torch is the easiest tool to get to the project, such as for welding a galvanized clothesline pole back together. There will also be times when the parts are too thin to dependably arc or MIG weld, such as when you have a toy, bicycle, or lawnmower handle that is bent, broken, or otherwise in need of welding. This chapter shows pictures of several people who are gas welding thin wall tubing for practice. In all cases, look at good welds that have been done by a factory or by a professional welder. Then try to copy the good welds as you see them.

The store advertised this pair of bottles as a welding set, but after reading the instructions that came with the unit, it's clear that the gas in the bottles would last only 10 to 15 minutes at brazing temperatures. The set is only capable of welding a single ¼-inch-diameter bolt together. This set would not be worth taking home.

The plastic handle broke completely, and most people would have thrown the yard cart away, but owning a gas welder saved the cart. A short piece of electrical conduit (EMT) was brazed to the flanges, which were bolted to the handle.

HINTS FOR GAS TORCH SOLDERING AND BRAZING

Two things must be considered when gas torch soldering and brazing. Solder melts at about 350 degrees Fahrenheit up to 500 degrees Fahrenheit, and the gas torch flame is about 6,200 degrees Fahrenheit. This means that you can't hold the torch to the metal to be soldered or else you will burn up or vaporize your project with the excess heat from the torch.

The second thing that must be remembered when gas or flame soldering is that the flux is usually scorched or burned by a direct flame. You will ruin the flux very quickly if you let the flame touch the flux. To properly flame solder, apply the heat to the metal and then apply the flux to the heated metal. In the case of flame soldering copper tubing fittings, it is best to flux the joint, but use a flux-cored solder. If you practice this method on some scraps of tubing and fittings, you will find that copper is really easy to flame solder. And practice makes perfect, or at least a lot better.

You can flame braze steel, sheet steel, galvanized steel, cast iron, brass, copper, aluminum, and do it very well and strong as long as you do not ever need to fusion weld it in the future.

The main reason you should never braze something that you may want to arc or MIG weld some day in the future is that braze metal, brass, silver, or aluminum will boil at the higher temperatures that are used for fusion welding. Aluminum brazing is one exception to this rule. Brazing aluminum and fusion welding aluminum are done at similar temperatures, usually within 100 to 200 degrees of each other.

Also, if you find the need to braze a brass pipe fitting or a brass pump housing, the temperatures for brazing and fusion welding are similiar, plus few companies will sell arc welding rod for brass. One minor exception is a special silicon-bronze bare rod for TIG brazing steel, brass, bronze, or stainless. If you own a TIG welder and want to use silicon-bronze rod for special projects, it will work well.

But if you have brazed a pipe frame and want to arc weld it later, it won't work. You will only fume and boil the brass and contaminate your weld because brass boils and evaporates at the melting point of steel and the higher flame temperature of a gas torch. A good rule is if you want to fusion weld it later, don't braze it now.

WHAT GOGGLES ARE BEST FOR GAS WELDING?

For many years, the goggles that were furnished with gas welding kits were two round lenses in frames connected with a leather strap or even a bead chain like on a sink stopper. These goggles were usually very dark, a No.7 to even a No.9 lens. You could hardly see how to weld with them, even in bright sunlight. Because of the dark lenses and cumbersome goggles, many people gave up on welding. Thankfully there have been improvements to the goggles.

Oxy-Acetylene welding flames do not produce radiation like arc welders. The gas flame light is bright and is like looking at a clear 200-watt light bulb, but there is no radiation from the flame. Therefore, you just need a light shade, such as a No.3 lens to weld. Look for a safety glasses-type lens that will fit over your prescription glasses. Most welding supply stores will have a "shaded visitor's safety glass" lens. You could even gas weld with a good pair of sunglasses, except that you need close-fitting glasses to protect against sparks and metal filings. But make sure that you wear eye protection for any welding process.

There are many people who need to wear prescription eyeglasses for reading and general vision. In many instances, these people remove their prescription glasses to weld because the kit-furnished goggles will not fit over their eyeglasses. They can not see well enough to weld, no more than they could see well enough to read. More than anything, take special care to find a good pair of safety green glasses to wear while welding. If you have been trying to weld without your eyeglasses, get yourself a good pair of No.3 safety glasses that will fit over your own glasses.

Most professional safety people do not recommend doing metal work, grinding, sanding, welding, and the like while wearing contact lenses. This is because a small piece of metal could get into your eye and become lodged under your contact lens. You should wear glasses, not contact lenses, when welding. The problem with bifocals and trifocals is that you may be looking at the weld sideways with the top part of your glasses with one eye and the bottom part of your glasses with the other eye. The result is often that you will see two weld puddles and you will not be able to tell which one to weld. Get yourself a pair of magnifying glasses for welding.

Fourteen-year-old Gregg Rocha uses a tip cleaner on an oxyacetylene torch before brazing a wire basket for an electric cart. Tip cleaners are a must for good welding, but they tend to wear the tip, which means the tips should be replaced every few dozen hours of welding.

Gregg is using Cronatron 30F brazing rod to repair a loose bracket on a wire basket. He's also using number 3 tint safety glasses, which fit very well over his prescription glasses. His brother, 11-year-old Dimetras Rocha, is looking over Gregg's shoulder.

A gas welder was used to braze the framing flanges to the EMT tubing, and the brazed assembly was bolted to the handle flange. This repair saved the yard cart from the dump. Be careful of toxic fumes when welding or brazing galvanized metal.

Brazing saved this antique cast-iron wheel from the scrap pile. Note the braze repairs on the vertical spoke near the hub, at the 2 o'clock position on the rim, and on the spoke near the hub on the 10 o'clock position. Grinding a vee at the break would have made a more sanitary braze repair.

Continue from page 70
can be silver or lead soldered, but a propane torch works best for this.

BRAZING WITH GAS

Brazing temperatures range from 800 to 1,200 degrees Fahrenheit. Remember that steel melts at temperatures much above that. Many metals can be brazed, including aluminum, copper, brass, stainless steel, cast iron, and mild steel. Don't try to braze chrome-moly or 4130-N steel because 4130 has a grain that will usually crack when the brass alloy heats it to brazing temperatures. There are as many alloys of brazing rod as there are alloys of metal. If you have any doubts about which brazing alloy will work best, don't ask your local welding supply dealer because they probably won't know. Call one of the companies listed in the appendix and ask the technical representative any questions you may have.

To braze mild steel, such as a bicycle frame, the best brazing rod is the flux-covered rod that your local welding supplier probably has in stock. Buy about 1 pound of the rod and keep it in a plastic tube to prevent moisture contamination. See Chapter 10 for a way to store flux-covered brazing rod. The flux coating can flake off if it gets wet or is handled roughly.

Brazing Procedure
- Make sure that all paint, rust, and oil have been removed from about a 1-inch area around where the braze joint will be. Scuffing or sanding the joint is a good preparation, but wipe off the sanding dust before brazing.
- Light the torch and adjust for a slightly carburizing flame, just past a neutral flame, for a flame that's cooler than neutral.
- Play the flame around the joint and on the steel, bring the color up to just dark red, then touch the metal with the rod to rub off some of the flux and start the brazing rod to flow onto the metal to "wet" it.

A southpaw is fusion welding a cluster of steel tubing in this photo. H. G. Frautschy of EAA Oshkosh is practicing his gas welding skills. He is wearing a full number 5 shade face shield over his prescription glasses. The tip cleaner is lying nearby and is ready for use, if needed.

- Absolutely do not get the steel base metal any hotter than medium red, because the brazing rod will begin to boil and repel the brass.
- For brazing cast iron, the procedure is the same as for steel, including cleaning and pre-heating before starting the braze joint.
- After brazing, if it's practical, put the part in a tub of water so the flux will soften and flake off. If you don't soak it in water for about 5 minutes, the flux will be like glass and will stay on the part for several years, continually flaking off. It's much tidier to let water remove the flux residue for you.
- Brazing steel can also be done with a bare brazing rod and powdered flux. Just heat the rod slightly with the torch and dip the rod into the powdered flux. The flux will stick to the heated rod, and the brazing will be the same as for coated rod.

Note: Do not attempt to fusion weld a part that has been brazed previously. This is because the lower temperature melting point of the braze will be much below the melting point of the base metal, and the *boiling point* of the braze rod will be lower than the melting point of the base metal. The braze will boil and contaminate the fusion weld severely.

FUSION WELDING WITH GAS

Remember that steel melts at 2,600 degrees Fahrenheit and that the oxyacetylene torch's flame is 6,200 degrees Fahrenheit. Fusion welding is a process in which two or more pieces of metal are joined into one metallurgically unified part. The gas flame makes a molten puddle on the parts, and then a similar small-diameter metal rod is placed into the molten puddle and melted off to complete the joining procedure. Add rod as many times as needed to make a sound weld seam.

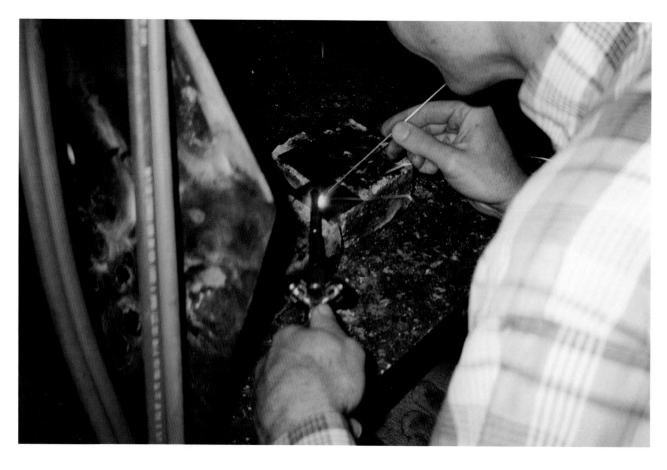

Yet another lefty is fusion welding a piece of steel sheet. If you are left handed, you can hold the torch in your left hand and the welding rod in your right hand. Gloves are not needed for light gas welding if you have a pair of pliers to pick up the hot metal.

A practice fusion weld of a steel tubing cluster is being completed by a right-handed gas welder. The torch flame is about 3 inches away from the weld so the weld puddle can be controlled and not melt through the metal.

Here is a fusion welded T section of thin 4130 steel aircraft tubing being held by pliers so the bare hands of the welder won't be burned. The weld exhibits a good, cool weld. A hot or burned-up weld would be grainier and more porous.

You should practice a lot on some scraps before you take on a serious welding project. Welding thin tubing like this is not easy, but once you master it, you can begin to really enjoy it. These practice welds are lumpy and incomplete.

It may not look like aluminum because it's so dirty, but this is an aluminum engine-oil pan from a Continental 6-cylinder engine. A steel braided hose has rubbed a long hole in the bottom of the oil pan. The torch is being held at a very flat angle to avoid melting an even larger hole while trying to repair the existing hole. A flux-core brazing rod is being used here.

It's important for you to know that fusion welding mild and 4130 steel parts does not require any flux. In fact, fluxing a steel fusion weld would create serious problems in the weld. Just make sure that the parts to be welded are clean and free of rust, paint, and oil. It's a good idea to remove any traces of mill scale before gas welding steel. Use a strip of sandpaper to clean the mill scale off, and wipe off all traces of sandpaper dust before welding.

Typical gas welding projects on the farm would be to weld an extension on a tailpipe, but be aware that modern car and truck exhaust systems are often made from aluminized or stainless steel. These coatings can be hard to gas weld, and you may need to MIG weld the newer exhaust systems.

Galvanized steel pipe and tubing can be fusion welded, but extra caution must be taken to avoid breathing the fumes from the heated galvanized metal. In this instance, a suction fan works well to rid the area of noxious gasses (see Chapter 2).

FUSION WELDING ALUMINUM WITH GAS

Remember that aluminum melts at 1,200 degrees Fahrenheit, and your gas welding torch produces 6,200 degrees Fahrenheit. It is entirely possible to fusion weld aluminum with an oxyacetylene torch if proper cleaning and fluxing procedures are adhered to. In one example of a farm and ranch aluminum welding job, we'll make repairs to aluminum irrigation pipe. Take a look at the fusion welding pictures of a Continental six-cylinder engine oil pan in this chapter. You have to forget about melting steel temperatures while welding aluminum. And remember that aluminum demands that you clean it and use flux for gas welding. Go to your local auto body shop paint store and buy a quart of aluminum prep to clean the parts prior to welding. Mix the aluminum prep with three parts water to one part DuPont aluminum prep and soak the parts for 1 hour prior to welding.

So, how do you weld aluminum with a gas torch? The trick is to manipulate the torch as needed to avoid aluminum's

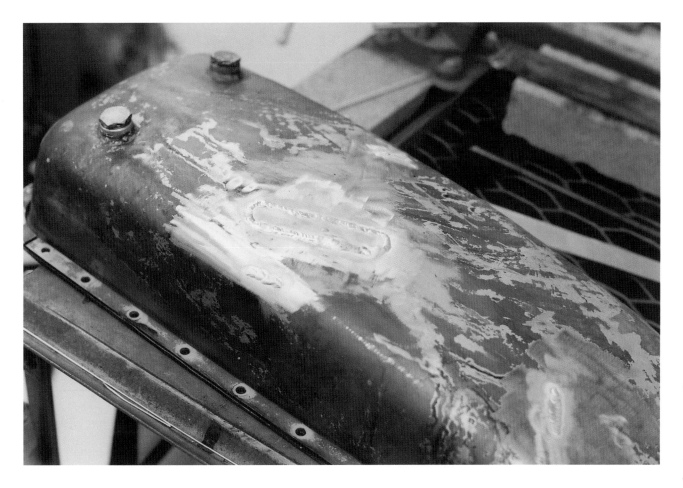

The aluminum 6-cylinder Continental engine-oil pan has been fusion welded with a flux-core brazing rod. A patch was placed over the hole in the pan. A brazing rod was used because the melting point was within 150 degrees of the oil pan's melting point. Another reason for using the flux-core rod was the convenience of the flux as opposed to mixing up a powdered flux.

boiling point of 4,450 degrees Fahrenheit. Lay the torch flatter and pull it away when you see the molten puddle getting too big. By doing this, you can do a good job welding aluminum. Remember that the 6,200-degree Fahrenheit flame is only the short blue flame near the tip, and the rest of the flame, which is about 8 inches long, is cooler as you get farther away from the torch tip.

FUSION WELDING STAINLESS STEEL WITH GAS

Stainless steel melts at 2,650 degrees Fahrenheit. As with welding aluminum, cleanliness and proper fluxing is part of the secret to making a good weld with a gas torch. But stainless steel has an extra problem with melting and fusing. It doesn't like to be heated and melted! One trick is to form small ⅛-inch flanges on each side of the part and melt the flange down without really heating the flat plate of stainless steel.

Another solution is to mix up some Solar Flux and coat the back side of the weld with the flux and follow the instructions on the flux can. See Chapter 9 for more on welding stainless steel. As opposed to fusion welding mild and 4130 steels, stainless steel absolutely must be welded by using a flux. See Chapter 10 for which Solar Flux to use when welding stainless steels.

HARD FACING STEEL WITH A GAS TORCH

This hard-facing process is similar to brazing. It applies to steel at a melting point of 1,300 to 1,400 degrees Fahrenheit. This special rod is a brand-name hard-facing rod, and it must be ordered from the manufacturer. Not many local welding supply houses will stock it. It comes in sizes of ⅛-inch diameter by 18-inches long, and 3/16-inch diameter by 18-inches long. It applies with an oxyacetylene torch set as for brazing. Among the many uses for this material are building up antique engine rocker-arm wear

HINTS FOR GAS WELDING ALUMINUM

Most people who are learning to weld aluminum, after they have learned to weld steel, will notice that the aluminum does not become red like steel does. Therefore when welding they suddenly see a smooth, shiny surface on the aluminum and "bang," the aluminum suddenly drops out and makes a big hole. When the surface starts to get shiny, that is the puddle you need for fusion welding aluminum. When you are welding steel, you have a much wider range of temperatures before you have a suitable puddle for fusion welding, but that is not the case with aluminum. Remember that aluminum melts at around 1,200 degrees Fahrenheit, so as you are fusion welding or brazing aluminum, watch the surface for a shiny spot. That is your puddle. When you see the shiny spot, be ready to pull the torch back to prevent "melt through." Once you get the hang of "the shiny spot," you will find that welding aluminum is a lot of fun.

Another special thing about welding or brazing aluminum is that the surface to be welded must be very clean compared to fusion welding steel. You can easily weld a rusty tailpipe, but you can't weld a corroded aluminum irrigation pipe. You must have the aluminum very clean. In the field, a wire brush, some aluminum prep acid, and clean water to flush off the acid is a must. A small, toothbrush-sized stainless steel brush works great for cleaning aluminum before welding. These special brushes are available at most welding supply stores and farm equipment stores that sell welding supplies.

PRACTICING GAS WELDING ON STEEL

A common mistake made by a lot of novice gas welders is trying to melt off the welding rod and letting it drop onto cold steel. You are right, that does not make a weld. You must first make a molten puddle on the parts you want to weld together, and then you put the welding rod into the already molten puddle of steel, letting the rod melt in the puddle. The puddle is supposed to melt the rod and the flame is only secondary to melting the rod. But, it is also correct that the flame will be utilized in making a completely fused and homogeneous weld.

One way to improve your gas welding steel skills is to practice making a puddle and maintain the puddle without putting the welding rod into the puddle. It may be a good idea for you to hold the welding rod behind you to avoid the urge to put rod onto a piece of steel that is not hot enough to be welded. In welding school you are taught to weld many small steel pieces together until you get it right, but that wastes your time and pieces of steel. Just get in there and weld something realistic, like a welding cart or a muffler to an exhaust pipe.

If you burn (melt) a hole in the metal, slow down and put the melted rod into the hole and puddle it all together. Doing that will teach you to not make any holes if you can avoid it. In fact, patching a hole or two will teach you how to control the heat and do a better job of welding.

The entire time you are gas welding, tell yourself that the weld goes where you point the torch. If you have a lump of weld metal that does not look pretty, it is okay to use the torch flame to melt and "push" the lump into a nice looking weld. The weld puddle is like a puddle of water on a table top. It flows by capillary action to the source of the heat, and in this case it is the flame of the weld torch.

surfaces, hardening clevises that wear easily, and putting a wear surface on post-hole diggers, shovels, picks, and other smaller tools. A commercial name is Cronawear 79, and the part number is CW-1027 for the ⅛-inch size.

You might be able to purchase a similar hard-facing rod from your local welding supplier, but be sure that it comes with a good set of application instructions.

CHAPTER 7
ARC WELDING: AC/DC CURRENT MACHINES

DIFFERENT KINDS OF ARC WELDERS

The arc welding machine is the backbone of the farm and ranch welding shop. There are many kinds of arc welding machines: some are old and some are brand new. In this chapter, we'll discuss a 20-year-old college student who built her dad some pipe corrals with her brother-in-law's old Wisconsin V-4-powered Lincoln portable arc-welding generator. But on the day that she was photographed for this book, she was using the very latest technology in inverter combination TIG and SAW machines, the Lincoln Invertec V205-T AC/DC welder.

If you already have an arc welder, you'll learn here how to properly use it, or maybe you'll learn that you would be better off trading it for a more modern piece of equipment. And remember that if you have a "good" arc welder, a "good" gas welder, and a 4-inch angle grinder, you can build and repair many things on your farm or ranch.

WELDING ROD SIZES AND TYPES

Most arc welding repairs on a farm are done with a standard stick of ⅛-inch diameter rod, AWS E-6011 or AWS E-7018. The 6011 rod is mild steel, all position, and is easy to start

A lot of the welding projects in this chapter were done with this Lincoln Electric Invertec V205-T AC/DC machine. It functions as a stick welder on either 110 or 220 volts without any changes to the machine. Just use a 110-volt adapter plug to adapt the 220-volt, 50-amp plug and plug it in. The machine figures out which voltage to use.

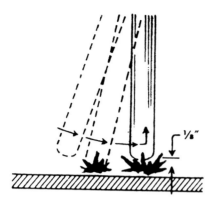

To strike an arc, scratch the end of the rod on the plate and then quickly raise the rod about 1/8 of an inch.

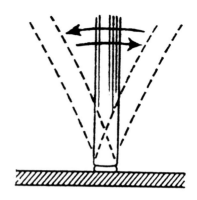

Should the rod stick or freeze, bend it from side to side while pulling upward on the rod holder.

To lay a weld bead, only two movements are used, downward and in the direction the weld is to be laid.

Watch the weld puddle to keep the slag from flowing in front of it, which would cause inclusions and gas pockets.

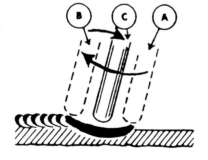

When starting a new rod, fill the crater by striking the arc at A, then moving to B, and back to C position.

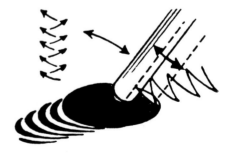

To widen the bead, work the rod from side to side slightly with a slow, zigzagging, crescent-shaped motion..

This drawing shows how you should hold the stick-welding stinger in order to start your first weld and all the welds you will do from now on. It also helps if you steady your right hand with your left hand. Reverse everything if you're left-handed. Author collection

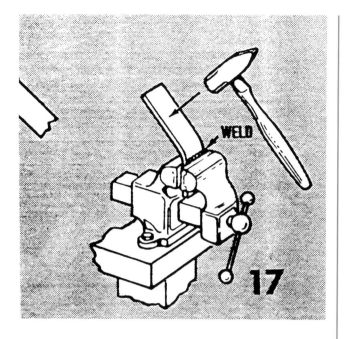

To test your welds, put the metal in a vise and hit it with a big hammer. If it bends and does not break, you did a good job! If you bend toward your weld rather than away as the drawing shows, it will better test the weld. Author collection

WELDER POLARITY

An inexpensive buzzbox welder with 220 volts and AC only is always an AC welding machine, and you must choose welding rod that is specified for AC compatibility.

A DC welding machine can weld on either polarity, DC negative or DC positive. Almost no arc welding is ever done with DC positive, because there would be very little heat and penetration in that mode. So you're either going to weld in AC or DC straight, negative, or reverse polarity. Straight, reverse, and negative all denote the same polarity. Positive or plus are the same polarity, but are seldom used. Just remember that the electrode holder is always on the straight or negative plug so you'll have better heat penetration.

an arc. It gives good penetration with either an AC or a DC welding machine. It's not as sensitive to aging in the box as low-hydrogen rods are, and its main drawback is that it produces a lot of spatter and tends to bury its slag in the weld bead. So it's not as strong as 7018 rod.

Commonly called lo-hi or low hydrogen, E-7018 is preferred for X-ray-quality welds. Lo-hi rod E-7018 rod is not particularly easy to use, especially for a beginning welder, but once you've gotten the hang of how it runs, you'll really like how it welds. The weld bead will be smooth, without spatter, and it will almost chip itself. A good bead on flat metal will allow the slag or cover to actually peel up and come off without any chipping. People will recognize that you're an accomplished welder if you can run a good bead with E-7018 rod. One important problem with E-7018 rod

This is a typical farm repair weld made with E-6013 welding rod with a diameter of 3/16-inch. The diameter of the weld rod is the biggest factor in determining the size of the finished weld. The plate with the hole in it is a patch plate reinforcement.

Twenty-year-old Leslie Abercrombie starts a weld bead on a disc cultivator on her family farm in New Mexico. Heavy leather gloves, a denim jacket, and denim pants protect her from the radiation of the weld and from the sparks and heat.

WELDING ROD NUMBERS

The American Welding Society (AWS) has a standard numbering system. The numbers on the rod specify the kind of rod and its intended use. Here are a few examples:

* E-7018—E means electrode for electric arc welding; is not to be used for TIG or GAS
  70 means 70,000-pounds tensile strength
  1 means position, this is an all-position rod
  8 means AC and DC rod polarity and can be used on any welding machine

* E-6011—E means electrode, for electric arc welding; is not to be used for TIG or GAS
  60 means 60,000-pounds tensile strength
  1 means position, this is an all-position rod
  1 means AC/DC rod polarity and coating

* E-6024—E means electrode for electric arc welding; is not to be used for TIG or GAS
  60 means 60,000 pounds tensile strength
  2 means flat position only
  4 means AC and DC rod

Leslie is holding the rod stinger with both hands for a steady weld bead. The welding machine is the Lincoln 205-T and is running on a 110-volt circuit in the nearby barn.

SUGGESTIONS FOR WELDING ROD STOCK

E-6010 and 5p rods are also called pipe-welding rod. They weld smoothly with very little spatter.

E-6011 is called dirty-welding rod because it will weld OK on rust, oil, and paint, and it has lots of spatter.

E-6013 is a very good rod for a home and farm workshop. It has no spatter and is a nice weld on flat or out-of-position work.

E-7018 is a high-quality rod and is a little harder to use, except in the flat position. It makes really nice welds.

There are specialty rods for cast iron, stainless steel, high-strength, cutting, bi-metals, hard-facing, and other metals.

is that it absorbs moisture very quickly. In one example, regulations at construction sites for nuclear reactors require that all E-7018 rod be placed in appropriate trash receptacles at the end of each 8-hour shift because the rod would become too contaminated by moisture to use even if it's kept in a heated rod-carrying oven. On the farm, you can keep the rod dry by placing it in a sealed can and heating it to 200 degrees Fahrenheit for 8 hours just before you use it.

WELDING ROD OVENS

If most types of welding rods are allowed to sit out and collect moisture, for even a week, it can be difficult to strike and maintain an arc. Often a pound of seemingly good rod will refuse to arc and run a bead if it's damp. The solution is to keep the rod in a sealed plastic canister. An old method was to put a lightbulb in a 5-gallon can and store the rods there, but the lightbulb can burn out, and the cost to light the bulb day and night was excessive. Make or buy a plastic rod-storage tube and heat the rod for 8 hours at 200 degrees in the kitchen oven just before welding.

Here's what Leslie's smile looks like under her helmet. Leslie won the helmet in an FFA welding contest when she was in high school.

Pueblo Pipe and Steel's business is fabricating steel-framed carports. These welded brackets are done in the flat position because it's much easier. Don't weld vertically if you can weld flat.

Your trusty cut-off saw is very useful for cutting standard 20-foot lengths of steel into sizes that you can use on your projects. It can save time if you make a simple drawing of your project before you start cutting and welding. Watch where those sparks go!

CLOTHING FOR ARC WELDING

If you will be doing a lot of overhead welding with a stick (arc) welder, then a good leather jacket that fully covers your upper torso and arms would be a good investment. New jackets cost around $50, but a denim shirt, pants, and jacket are typically adequate body protection. It would be a good idea to bind up the ankles of your denims so the spatter won't fall into your shoes and socks. Getting a hot spark in your shoe or down your chest is not a good thing! Leather gloves are important, too. The newer self-darkening arc welding helmets are really nice for beginners and part-time welders, but an older number 11 to 13 shade lens in a regular helmet will give you less eye strain for day-in and day-out welding. Many welders complain about eye itch after welding with a darkening-lens helmet all day long. Finally, a welder's cap is good protection against sparks falling in your hair and causing scalp burns, especially for overhead welding.

PRACTICE WELDING

A good idea for all welders is to practice for a few minutes before starting a serious project. Get a short piece of 2-inch angle steel or a piece of steel the size of a dinner plate, at least ¼-inch thick, to practice on. Then review the illustrations in this chapter that demonstrate how to make good welds. A tip for all welders is to turn the amperage up to at least 120 amps when striking your first few arcs. This will keep you from sticking the welding rod until you become proficient at starting and maintaining a steady arc. Most beginners and "rusty" welders tend to stick the rod for the first few starts. Temporarily turning up the amps will help you get in sync with the welding arc.

ADVANCED WELDING

Try to weld in the flat position as much as possible. You'll just make it hard on yourself if you try to weld in positions other than flat. Your welds will look a lot better and will be

ARC WELDING: AC/DC CURRENT MACHINES

87

Sections of 1½-inch square steel tubing have been cut to the proper lengths for making a pipe or ladder rack for an old Ford pickup. Once the tubing is cut to exact lengths, it's easy to build a structure as long as you know where each piece is supposed to fit.

stronger if you take your time and fit each weld as perfectly as possible. For metals that are thicker than ¼-inch, you'll need to bevel the edges so the weld bead can penetrate and give as much weld in the joint as the metal is thick, plus a crown and some weld sticking through on the backside of the weld. Beveling the edge to be welded is a good rule for almost all types of weld joints over ¼-inch thick.

OVERHEAD WELDING

For overhead welding, use an E-6013 welding rod because it does not make as much spatter as E-6011 rod, and you don't want any more spatter and sparks falling on you than is necessary for welding. It's a little easier to make overhead welds if you turn the amps down about 10 percent less than what you would have used for a flat weld, because gravity will tend to make the weld puddle fall out. A cooler puddle will solidify faster. After you start the arc, hold the rod a little closer than you would for flat welding. If you see the puddle starting to droop down, either push it back up or flick it out of the weld and stop and wait about 5 seconds

for the puddle to cool before re-starting the arc. Practice on a piece of scrap before actually starting the actual weld.

PIPE WELDING

Pipe welding, such as building a pipe corral or fence, is all out-of-position welding. You are always welding uphill, downhill, or overhead, with very little flat welding. Experiment with several welding rods to see which number will suit your project the best. Certain welding rod manufacturers call some of their welding rods "fast-freeze" because they solidify more quickly than standard rod. Try a pound of fast-freeze rod for pipe welding, but the old standard number 5p rod is very good for this kind of welding.

VERTICAL AND HORIZONTAL WELDING

Vertical and horizontal stick welding are a lot easier to do properly if you remind yourself that the puddle goes wherever you point the rod. For instance, if you must weld a horizontal seam in a steel plate or piece of angle steel, the puddle will sag due to gravity. If you just point the rod toward the

A 175-amp stick welder is being used to assemble the sides of the new rack. A 110-volt MIG welder was tried, but it would not penetrate the 0.090-inch steel tubing, so the stick welder was used instead. Notice that the welder steadies his right hand with the fingers of his left hand.

TYPES OF WELDING RODS

There are special welding rods out there called Jet Rod and EasyStrike. Both of these welding rods are actually a variation of the E-6013 welding rod, a mild steel rod that welds nice and clean and is easy to strike an arc. It is common for companies to rename a welding rod so that they can obtain customer loyalty for their seemingly better welding rod. The fact is that the American Welding Society (AWS) sets standards for most welding rods, and most companies will still post the AWS number somewhere on the package, although it will be in fine print.

In the case of the EasyStrike welding rod made by MG Industries, the recommendation is for this rod to be used in auto body work, sheet metal work, bicycle frame repairs, and four-wheel-drive, off-road vehicle repairs. It is also to be used for quick repairs in place of brazing, TIG welding, or even MIG welding. This rod has a 1/16-inch diameter and is used on the low voltage, 110 volt machines and at less than 40 amps, which is perfect for a lot of jobs around the farm or ranch.

In most farm applications, you will find good use for about four or five different welding rod numbers and two or three sizes, with the 1/8-inch diameter rod being the most common. One local farm and ranch operator actually keeps their welding rods in the kitchen to keep them dry and protected from damage, but that is not necessary if you keep your various sizes and numbers in sealed plastic containers in the welding area. See Chapter 9 for special welding rods that are helpful around the farm or ranch.

This is a good example of shade-tree welding. It's OK to weld on the grass as long as it isn't dry and flammable. Note the wood used to level and hold the square tubing off the grass and to level the whole frame.

seam as you've been doing with flat welding, you'll get a saggy weld. Practice for a few minutes before welding the real parts, and use the E-6013 weld rod for vertical welding.

Point the rod a little up as you weld the seam, and try reducing the amps from 90 to 81, about a 10 percent decrease. Regularly practice welding horizontally, and weave the weld bead up and come back down and push the puddle back into place. Repeat this over and over again until you have a non-sagging weld bead. Nobody can make a perfect horizontal bead on the first try. You must try it, then stop and look at your weld and figure out what you need to do to improve the next time you run a horizontal bead.

Vertical-up welding is harder to do than vertical-down welding. The molten puddle wants to sag toward the floor due to gravity, and if you are pointing the rod down to lead the puddle as you do in flat welding, the puddle will be harder to control. First try vertical-down welding so you'll be able to push the puddle back into the weld seam. Also

keep in mind that it's more important to watch what the puddle is doing than to watch the arc. Again, the puddle goes wherever you point the rod.

CONTROLLING WARPAGE WHILE WELDING

One way to control warpage is to stitch weld. Look at the illustration in this chapter to see how stitch welding is done. You merely weld for a fraction of an inch, then skip to a cooler part of the seam, weld another short weld, and continue to do the same until you have completed your weld. Let the part cool for a few minutes and go back and weld in between your previous welds. Be sure to chip your welds after they cool and before starting a new stringer weld.

WELDING THIN TO THICK METAL

There will be a number of projects that require you to weld sheet metal to angle steel, pipe, or wire to pipe. This can be a lot of fun once you get the hang of it. The secret is to start

Here a pair of vise-grip pliers are used to provide a clamp surface so a carpenter's clamp can hold the side of the frame together for welding. If you don't have things lined up before you tack weld them, your welds will not be accurate and sound.

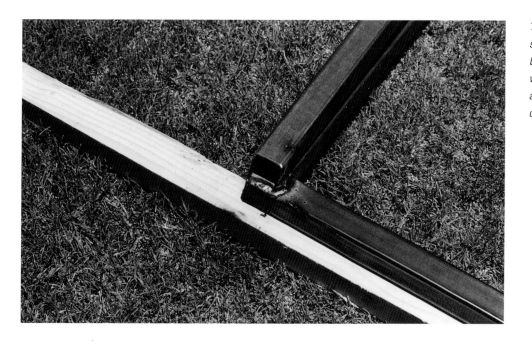

The right front corner of the square-tube ladder rack has been welded with E-6013 welding rod. Some smoke is apparent, but wire brushing will clean that off.

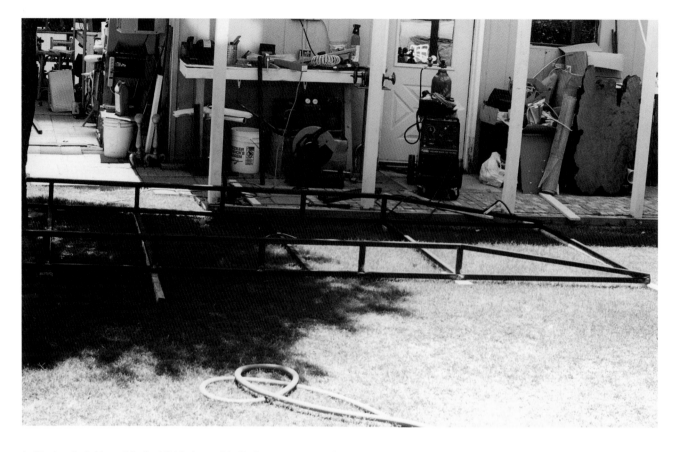

In this view, the ladder rack is about finished, except for the four corner posts and some angle bracing. Next it will be flipped over and attached to the four posts. If the drawing is right, it should fit the truck.

an arc weld puddle near the thin piece of metal and let the puddle flow over to the thin metal. Once you have the process figured out, you'll find that you probably don't need to weld 100 percent of the length of the thin piece. Just figure that you are riveting the thin piece to the thick piece. A good welding engineer would never ask for sheet metal to be welded to thick angle in a 100 percent weld. The engineer would ask for a stitch weld.

WELDING FUMES ARE HAZARDOUS

It is known that welding fumes can contribute to Parkinson's Disease, which affects the nervous system and causes uncontrolled shaking. It has been proven that welders who constantly breathe arc welding fumes are 10 times more likely to develop Parkinson's Disease than people who are not welders by trade. Be careful and do not allow the smoke and fumes from the arc flow around your helmet and face. The fumes can also cause chemical bronchitis.

APPLYING HARD-FACING ROD TO STEEL

Most of the time, hard facing is applied when dozer blades and plowshares have been worn down and need to be replaced. The line drawings in this chapter illustrate the procedure to replace the blades. A typical project in high school welding class is to run a series of weld beads side-by-side and over the top of each other to build up a metal surface that resembles a worn dozer blade. Be sure to chip the flux off and wire brush the weld before you make the next weld pass. A very good hard-facing rod is Cronatron Cronawear Eagle number 7355. Other local suppliers may also have a generic hard-facing rod.

ARC WELDING CAST IRON

One of the so-called mysteries of farm equipment repair is the question of how to dependably weld cast iron. If you use the correct welding rod and procedure, this is fun to do. An excellent cast-iron arc-welding rod is Cronatron Cronacast

The job is done! The pickup is ready to go to town and haul a load of lumber and a few pieces of pipe. The new rack and pickup both need a good coat of paint. Rust-Oleum works pretty well in all climates, and primer would help, too.

An angle brace is being added to each of the four corner posts. Large metal clothespin-type clamps work very well for holding the corner braces while they are being tack welded. Some "out-of-position" welding will be done to weld the braces.

1-1/2 INCH

The owner of Pueblo Pipe and Steel has decided to build a handy enclosed trailer for his new Miller Bobcat portable 225-amp gasoline-driven welder/generator. Having a big supply of all kinds and sizes of angle and tubing is great when building a farm trailer like this one. Pueblo Pipe and Steel

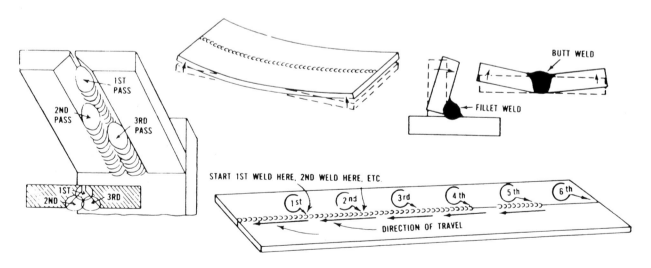

In the drawing at the left, you can see the proper sequence for running three passes of weld in an overhead position, which is the same thing you would do in the flat position. In the middle drawing, you can see what will happen if you weld a seam without stitching it. It bends from the concentrated heat. On the right, you can see that the weld bead will "pull" the metal if you don't stitch weld first. The bottom drawing shows how to stitch weld and avoid heat bending the metal. Author collection

In the drawing on the left, the welding rod is moved in the indicated directions for vertical-down and vertical-up welds. The drawing in the center shows a good one-pass weld on thin material, with some bead showing on the backside of the weld. The drawing on the right shows the same weld bead pass sequence used in flat and overhead welding. Author collection

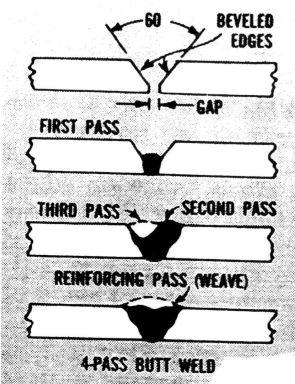

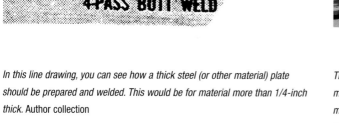

In this line drawing, you can see how a thick steel (or other material) plate should be prepared and welded. This would be for material more than 1/4-inch thick. Author collection

This is a good project for a rainy day when you can't be in the field. A lathe and milling machine table was built out of 2-inch angle iron and fitted for a factory-made toolbox so that all the lathe tools can be stored out of the dust. A side shelf can store saws, sanders, and grinders.

Leslie shows how she welded the thinner 4-inch concrete reinforcing grate to the thicker 2 1/2-inch pipe railing. Just start an arc on the pipe and let the puddle run onto the wire. Those goats will never escape now!

number 211, and it can even be used with a 225-amp AC-only buzzbox welding machine, but it works best with a good 175- to 200-amp DC machine set on DCRP. Cast-iron welding has been popular for about 50 years, but it requires some special processes, such as pre-heating and peening after welding. The welding rod that works the best for cast iron is called Ni-Rod. Cronatron 211 rod is used in the illustrations in Chapter 9. Be sure to read the welding rod manufacturer's instructions before attempting to repair a cast-iron part.

CUTTING STEEL, CAST IRON, ALUMINUM, AND MANY METALS WITH ARC ROD

Once you try this special cutting rod, you'll probably find many uses for it around the farm, ranch, or vineyard. Tasks such as cutting off rusty or rounded nuts, piercing holes in any kind of metal except magnesium, and cutting through old metal structures where a gas torch would be too difficult to use, can easily be completed with the cutting rod. The cutting rod demonstrated in Chapter 9 is a Cronatron Cronacut Eagle number 1100. This special rod will make

your farm life a lot easier. It will also chamfer, gouge, and sever metal parts that your gas cutting torch will not faze. There are other brands of cutting rods, but most are inferior to the one illustrated in Chapter 9.

PREHEATING BEFORE WELDING

Always preheat any metal over 1/4-inch thick before welding. Metals, steel especially are very sensitive to temperature. Don't try to weld metal that is outside in freezing temperatures. You will make cracks if you try it. Even aluminum will weld better when it is pre-heated to around 200 to 350 degrees Fahrenheit.

This rule of thumb applies to all weldable metal including aluminum, stainless steel, and regular carbon steel. Parts that are in excess of 1/4-inch thick, such as up to 1-inch thick, may require several minutes of preheating before welding. In the nuclear power industry, large pipe sections of 4 inches in diameter, with wall thicknesses of 1½ inch, are preheated to 400 degrees Fahrenheit for 8 hours prior to welding the first pass. This preheating is done with large,

In New Mexico, bare steel pipe rusts faster than in a more humid climate because of the dirt and dust in the air when it rains. It's not acid rain, but mineral rain. This horse corral is new and needs a coat of Rust-Oleum pretty quick!

At Horseman's Park, owned by Brandy and Robert Samuell, this recently built steel-pipe corral shows the E-6011 welding rod weld bead and the innovative gate-hinge design. Phosphoric acid and water are needed to prep this corral for paint.

Again in the background is the 12,000-foot Sierra Blanca Mountain, and in the foreground is a fence made out of welded pipe and hog wire. This will make a very good fence that will last a long time.

A close-up of the fence shows that the hog wire wasn't welded to the pipe, it was wired to the steel posts. This fence was painted with rust-resistant paint shortly after it was built, which saved some extra work.

Here a 110-volt arc welding machine is being used to stick weld a luggage rack on a well-used ATV. The welding machine will work for this and thinner material, but not for ¼-inch and thicker material.

Another ATV needs its muffler bracket welded. A stick welder was the best machine for this quick job because it took less time getting ready than any of the other types of welding machines.

Left: This typical five-row cultivator on the Abercrombie farm in Tularosa, New Mexico, is in need of some plowshare repair and hard-facing work. Note the broken plowshare in the foreground. Above: The top corner of this plowshare is broken off, which will create a bad furrow. The solution is to fabricate a replacement wing and weld it onto the plow. Hard facing the plow would be best done at this time, too.

8

Lay the weld beads about 1 inch apart. Remove the slag and examine each weld before starting the next.

9

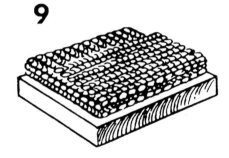

A pad of weld metal is built up by running a series of beads in layers at right angles to each other.

Practice running weld beads on a piece of scrap metal before you start welding on hard-facing material. The beads that you should run are shown in the drawings. Author collection

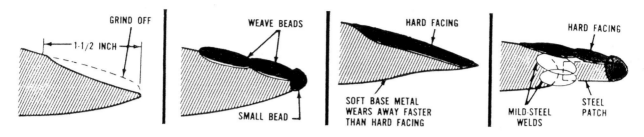

In the series of four drawings, the proper procedure for hard facing worn plowshares is shown. In some extreme cases, you may have to replace the metal with patches before adding hard-facing material. Author collection

commercial electric heating blankets that are not practical on a farm or ranch. This is where that oxy-acetylene torch with a rosebud tip comes in handy.

If you need to preheat a rather thick piece of metal, such as a broken front axle on a trailer, then you need to bring the temperature up to at least 200 to 350 degrees and hold it there for several minutes before you attempt to arc weld. There are many instances on the farm when a breakdown can be costly and prevent you from getting your work done. Being able to weld a repair that stays repaired is very important.

MULTIPLE PASSES OF WELD BEAD

Have you always assumed that you weld the metal once and then it is done? Not so. If the metal to be welded is thicker than the diameter of your welding rod, you must run enough weld bead passes to bring the weld up to more than

ARC WELDING HINTS

- Gravity helps make good welds. Therefore, try to weld everything in the horizontal or flat positon if possible. Turn the project over to make the welds more accessible. Most professional welding shops have positioners that try to get the weld structure up and flat so the welder can create sound, good welds. This is one secret to making strong welds.
- Run-off tabs help keep sound welds right to the edge of a part or assembly. These tabs can be made of scraps of the same metal that you are welding. Tack them to the edge where the weld bead ends and cut or grind them off once the weld is completed.
- Use smaller diameter electrodes when you are having to weld out-of-position joints. This will help you decrease the size of the weld puddle (see gravity tip above) and aid in creating a better weld. But this means that you will likely need to make more welding passes than with a larger diameter welding rod.
- Oscillate the welding rod to help make a larger pass of weld. This means that you can cover more area of the weld joint by weaving the rod, but you must be cautious and not include or cover slag when you are weaving or oscillating the rod and the arc. You must push the slag ahead of the weld puddle when you oscillate the rod.
- Don't coil the welding stinger cable or the ground cable while you are welding, especially when welding in AC current, because coiling the cables will act as a transformer and cause inductive losses of power at the welding arc. The amps you set on the machine will be a lot lower at the arc. Sometimes it helps to make a cable coil around a short piece of 6-inch steel pipe to make the machine weld at lower amps.
- Use extension cords only for the input and not on the ground or stinger cables. This will give you an arc with better control and penetration. In this chapter, you can see an arc welder at work that is using a 100 foot, 110 volt extension cord and it still is welding okay.
- Use a volt meter to find out if you have the voltage required for your welder. A common problem is when you are welding with a 220 volt machine and the line voltage is only 195 volts. Or sometimes a generator may not be producing the required voltage.

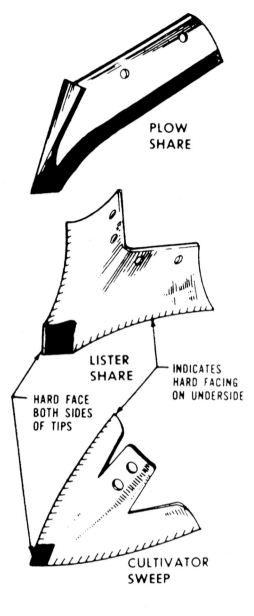

PLOW
SHARE

LISTER
SHARE

INDICATES
HARD FACING
ON UNDERSIDE

HARD FACE
BOTH SIDES
OF TIPS

CULTIVATOR
SWEEP

CULTIVATOR
SHOVEL

In the accompanying drawings, you can see where the new hard-facing welding rod should be added. But you can also decide this by looking at where the metal has been worn away by the dirt and rocks in the field. Author Collection

As long as you are going to be in the arc welding business on the farm or ranch, you need a bottle of Eye-Ease drops for those times when your eyes get just a little arc flash. These eye drops have an expiration date, so expect to buy a bottle every couple of years and throw the old bottle away, used or not.

the thickness of the part being welded. Check the drawings in this chapter for how to make more than one weld pass on a cracked or new weld.

CHIP AND WIRE BRUSH BETWEEN PASSES

Slag inclusions in your weld can cause cracks and failures. Make sure that you chip and use a wire brush with each pass. Do not try to chip the slag off too soon after you make the weld. Wait until the weld cools to about 400 degrees Fahrenheit before you try to chip and use a wire brush. The slag is there for a purpose. It covers and protects the weld bead from atmospheric contamination. If you want to experiment, try making an arc weld with a clean piece of bare wire or rod, but you can't weld very well this way.

The slag will chip off a lot cleaner and the weld will be better protected when you wait a few minutes after running the bead before you chip the slag off. That is why quality welding takes a little longer. Use a Tempil marker to make sure the metal is cool enough to chip and brush away.

INTERPASS TEMPERATURES

The interpass temperatures are more important when welding low carbon steel than it is when welding mild steel, but most of the time you really don't know how much carbon content the steel has in it. The best approach is to allow the metal to cool to 400 degrees Fahrenheit between weld bead passes. The reason for this very important temperature is easily seen when you study the Tempil chart on page 53 of this book. On the chart you will see that steel takes on certain atomic changes when it is heated to a certain temperature, usually still in the non-red heat zone. This atomic change causes the grain of the steel to form large crystals that become like ice crystals. The crystalization causes cracking in the area affected by the welding heat. You will have better welds all around if you take it slower and let your welds cool sufficiently before welding more passes. Use an Tempil marker to check your interpass temperatures and keep them around 400 degrees Fahrenheit.

CHAPTER 8
MIG WELDING, GAS, AND FLUX CORE

AN EASY KIND OF WELDING?

A lot of people think that a MIG welder will be just the ticket for farm and ranch repairs, because all you have to do is point the gun at the weld area and squeeze the trigger. That is very wrong! There's a lot more to MIG welding than first meets the eye. Often, a person who buys a simple buzzbox welder to stick-weld with, will have his machine working many hours before the person who buys one of those "simple-to-operate" MIG welders. There are some super-cheap MIG welders that can be purchased for under

This little 125-amp MIG welder is okay for sheet metal and for tailpipe material, but it will not weld 0.090-inch wall square tube as for the pickup ladder rack in Chapter 7. A higher-amp machine, such as 175 amps, would be better.

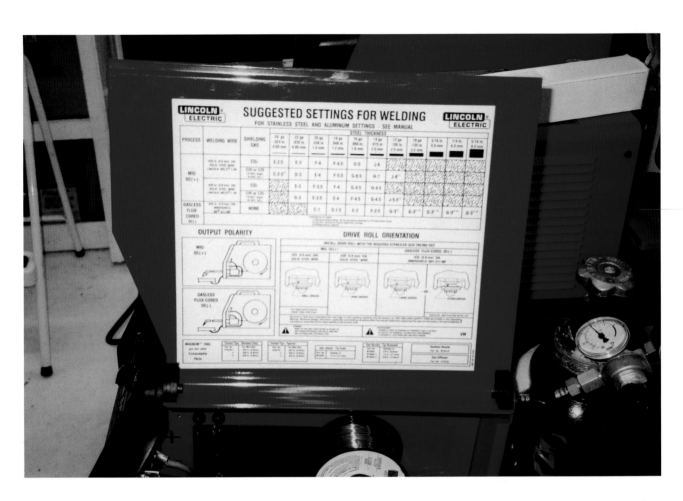

Inside the side door of the Lincoln SP-125 PLUS welder is a chart that gives a good starting point for each thickness of metal you might weld with the machine. But it won't weld 5/16-inch steel, as shown here, except with flux-core wire.

This Millermatic 175-amp machine is a 220-volt unit and cannot be operated on 110-volt house current. But at 175 amps, this machine is big enough to weld angle steel for a trailer frame, as long as the section of the angle is no more than 1/4-inch thick. Courtesy Valley Welding Supply

The 2-pound spool of wire will last a long time on this SP-125 welder. Another spool is ready to be used when the first spool is depleted. The polarity of the machine is easy to change with the two wing nuts at the far left side.

$120 from mail-order catalogs, but these units can barely weld a couple of baked bean cans together. They are little more than a short circuit in a small box.

SIZE IS IMPORTANT

Even some well-known manufacturers sell weak MIG welders. These weaker machines are only suitable for welding car fenders and tailpipes. They won't weld a frame for a trailer, even though the chart on the side of the MIG welding machine may show that you can set the machine at a certain amperage and wire-feed speed for 3/16-inch steel or aluminum. Most small name-brand MIG welders can be set up for welding aluminum, but not very well. The machines that sell for under $600 will easily tangle the soft aluminum wire. You really need a spool-gun type welder to adequately weld aluminum. A picture of a spool gun is shown near the end of this chapter.

A farm or ranch welding shop should have at least a 175-amp MIG welder, but a 250-amp welder would be much better. One really big improvement in MIG welders is how they've come down in size and weight. MIG welders were 400-pound giants just a few years ago, and now a good machine—like a Lincoln SP-175, 2- to 175-amp, 220-volt machine—can weigh as little as 60 pounds. One of the best pieces of advice I can offer when buying a MIG welding machine is to try it before you buy it. If it won't weld tailpipes, you don't want it.

ARE MIG WELDERS COMPLICATED?

MIG welders are actually more complicated than a straight plain-stick welder. You can't just plug them in, put in a roll of wire, and expect them to work correctly. You have to study the instruction book and spend some time making the correct adjustments. Here are some facts on MIG welders:

- GMAW stands for Gas Metal Arc Welding, which means that a shielding gas is needed to protect the weld.

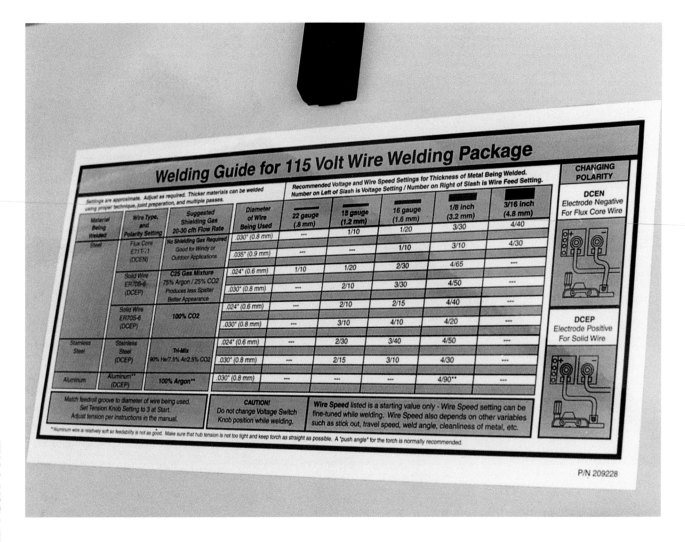

Welding Guide for 115 Volt Wire Welding Package

Settings are approximate. Adjust as required. Thicker materials can be welded using proper technique, joint preparation, and multiple passes.

Recommended Voltage and Wire Speed Settings for Thickness of Metal Being Welded. Number on Left of Slash is Voltage Setting / Number on Right of Slash is Wire Feed Setting.

Material Being Welded	Wire Type, and Polarity Setting	Suggested Shielding Gas 20-30 cfh Flow Rate	Diameter of Wire Being Used	22 gauge (.8 mm)	18 gauge (1.2 mm)	16 gauge (1.6 mm)	1/8 inch (3.2 mm)	3/16 inch (4.8 mm)
Steel	Flux Core E71T-11 (DCEN)	No Shielding Gas Required. Good for Windy or Outdoor Applications	.030" (0.8 mm)	---	1/10	1/20	3/30	4/40
			.035" (0.9 mm)	---	---	1/10	3/10	4/30
	Solid Wire ER70S-6 (DCEP)	C25 Gas Mixture 75% Argon / 25% CO2 Produces less Spatter Better Appearance	.024" (0.6 mm)	1/10	1/20	2/30	4/65	---
			.030" (0.8 mm)	---	2/10	3/30	4/50	---
	Solid Wire ER70S-6 (DCEP)	100% CO2	.024" (0.6 mm)	---	2/10	2/15	4/40	---
			.030" (0.8 mm)	---	3/10	4/10	4/20	---
Stainless Steel	Stainless Steel (DCEP)	Tri-Mix 90% He/7.5% Ar/2.5% CO2	.024" (0.6 mm)	---	2/30	3/40	4/50	---
			.030" (0.8 mm)	---	2/15	3/10	4/30	---
Aluminum	Aluminum** (DCEP)	100% Argon**	.030" (0.8 mm)	---	---	---	4/90**	---

Match feedroll groove to diameter of wire being used. Set Tension Knob Setting to 3 at Start. Adjust tension per instructions in the manual.

CAUTION! Do not change Voltage Switch Knob position while welding.

Wire Speed listed is a starting value only - Wire Speed setting can be fine-tuned while welding. Wire Speed also depends on other variables such as stick out, travel speed, weld angle, cleanliness of metal, etc.

**Aluminum wire is relatively soft so feedability is not as good. Make sure that hub tension is not too tight and keep torch as straight as possible. A "push angle" for the torch is normally recommended.

CHANGING POLARITY

DCEN Electrode Negative For Flux Core Wire

DCEP Electrode Positive For Solid Wire

P/N 209228

Another brand of MIG welder is a Hobart machine that also runs on 110-volt house current. This chart shows what the machine is capable of welding at 125 amps. It has its limitations, too.

- FCAW stands for Flux Core Arc Welding, which means that a flux core in the wire provides protection to the weld.
- Weld protection means that the molten metal is protected from oxygen, hydrogen, and other atmospheric gasses.
- Most nonprofessional welders just say "MIG, gas, or flux." It is easier to remember.
- A MIG welder that is set up for gas shielding can weld either steel or aluminum wire by changing the shielding gas. Aluminum requires pure argon for shielding, and steel requires a 75 percent argon and 25 percent CO_2 gas mix. The aluminum wire should have a special low-drag inner liner cable in the gun cable. The polarity of the gun must be changed to weld with flux core wire after welding with gas shielding.

- A MIG welder that's only set up for flux-cored wire can't weld aluminum.

MORE ADJUSTMENTS NEEDED

To adjust the wire rollers so they will roll the wire to the gun properly but not wear out prematurely, put the gun on a piece of wood or on the concrete floor, pull the trigger, and slowly tighten the wire roller until the wire pushes the gun back with about 3 or 4 pounds of pressure, then stop adjusting.

Keep a pair of side-cutting pliers in your back pocket to clip back the wire that sticks out after making a weld bead. The ball of metal on the wire will contaminate your weld. There will be many times when your wire will be sticking out way too much. You want about ½ inch of fresh wire sticking out to start a good weld.

MIG WELDING, GAS, AND FLUX CORE

This welder in the flaming hood is holding the MIG gun in his left hand and guiding it with his right hand. MIG welding is a two-handed skill. The large chain hook indicates that the unit he is welding on will be lifted and rotated to make welding it easier. Courtesy Miller Electric Company, Inc.

MIG WELDING, GAS, AND FLUX CORE

A Miller 175-amp MIG machine is used to do a weld repair on the tongue of this baler. Note that the wire power cable is as straight and free of tangles as possible to keep the wire moving smoothly. Always make sure that your wire cable is free of kinks and knots. Courtesy Miller Electric Company, Inc.

Before starting your weld, read the chart for the thickness of metal you're welding, and adjust the amps and wire-feed speed to exactly what the chart calls for. Don't try to adjust by ear, but you can fine-tune by ear.

Fine-tune your MIG weld by adjusting the speed knob to get a sound like bacon frying in a skillet from the weld. Don't adjust the amps knob, just the speed.

MAKING A GOOD MIG WELD

- Hold the MIG gun with your dominant hand and steady it with your other hand so you can make the weld bead go where it needs to go.
- Don't look directly at the back of the gun; you won't be able to see the weld puddle.
- Look at the side of the weld so you can see the puddle clearly through the smoke if it is flux core.
- If you can't see the weld puddle, you can't make a good weld. Look at the side of the weld puddle.
- Make sure that the entire gun cable is as straight as possible, with no kinks to brake or stop the wire.
- Do not stand on the weld gun cable because it will stop the wire.

SWITCHING OVER TO FCAW

You will need a small kit to convert your gas-shield welder to use flux-core wire. This kit includes a different gasless nozzle and a different liner for the gun cable. It will also be necessary to change the drive roll to fit the larger wire.

A Miller 175 MIG welder is running flux-core wire, as evidenced by the amount of smoke coming off the welding. The heavy I-beams require a lot of penetration, so flux-core was used instead of gas-shielded wire. Courtesy Miller Electric Company, Inc.

The instruction manual and machine will both have instructions on how to do it.

MIG WELDING TECHNIQUES

After an hour or more of welding, the gun nozzle will usually get plugged up with spatter. There are a couple of solutions to the spatter problem. One solution is an anti-spatter spray. Another solution is a pint-size jar of welding jelly that you dip the nozzle into. Both these solutions will make the spatter much easier to scrape off the nozzle cup. Spatter will disrupt the weld protection and cause weld contamination.

Copper-coated welding wire will flake off and plug up the liner in the cable after a number of hours of welding. You can take the cable off the machine, shake it, and blow it out with an air gun. After a number of cleanings, you'll need to replace the liner, and possibly the whole cable.

USING EXTENSION CORDS WITH A MIG WELDER

There will be times when the objects you need to weld are not near your welder. It is possible to hook up an extension cord to the power inlet plug and move the machine closer

109

It's not exactly a farm welding project, but these numerous bronze boat propellers are being welded to repair the nicks in the props by using a bronze wire product. Almost any wire composition can be welded with MIG. Ask your supplier for the metal wire you want. Courtesy Miller Electric Company, Inc.

to the work. If you are using a 110 volt machine, you can plug it into a grounded duplex outlet as long as you use a heavy-duty extension cord of less than 50 feet long. A longer extension cord will significantly reduce the volts for the welding machine.

Plug a volt meter into a socket at the input lead to the welder. An RV store volt meter will work in this configuration. These meters are handy for a lot of projects around the farm because they give you an instant reading of actual voltage, even while you are welding. The meters usually read from 95 up to 135 volts. One good brand of line voltage monitor is Tempo. These meters or monitors are rather accurate and will let you know if you have too low a voltage to make welding practical. It is normal for the voltage to drop about 5 to 10 volts from no welding to welding action, but the volt meter should not drop below 100 volts for a 110 volt machine (a 10 percent drop). If you are welding with a 220 volt circuit and a 220 volt machine, the drop still should not be more than 10 volts.

These line voltage monitors are so handy that you might want to use them for many other types of power tools such as grinders, skill saws, and electric soldering irons. Plug one into each socket in the shop area and leave them plugged in. You may find that your local power company does not produce stable power. In many areas, power companies allow the output power to vary from 100 volts up to 130 volts and the power can fluctuate at different times during the day and night. If you find this, you can call the power company and often it will do something to stabilize the power output.

WHY DOES POWER VOLTAGE VARIATION MATTER?

For example, if you are trying to make a delicate weld and suddenly you blow it, so to speak, it may not be your fault at all. If you have your welder set at 30 amps and the power goes from 105 to 125 volts instantly, you may burn a hole in your project because the power into your machine went up by 18 percent. It was not your fault. For delicate welding jobs, watch for a trend in the local power settings before you start the welding project. If the power is stable, you are in luck and at least you don't need to worry about the heat your welder is producing.

MIG WELDING, GAS, AND FLUX CORE

If you plan to do much aluminum welding with your MIG machine, you should try one of these spool guns that only has to push the soft aluminum wire from the head of the gun to the weld, which is about 9 inches, instead of the entire length of the power cord as in a standard MIG welder. It's called a Millennium MIG Spoolmate.
Courtesy Miller Electric Company, Inc.

WHAT DOES "DUTY CYCLE" MEAN TO WELDERS?

All electric welding machines are rated for a certain "duty cycle." This means that for a 20 percent duty cycle, in any one 10 minute welding period, the machine can only weld 2 minutes and then the machine must rest and cool for 8 minutes. Shutting off the power does not count. The welder must run and cool with the internal fan built into the machine. Often a good welding machine will be rated at 60 or 80 percent, but at the lower power settings. There are very few welding machines that can weld at 100 percent duty cycle, and this applies to commercial, manufacturing duty machines.

Most MIG and arc welders are rated at 60 percent at the lower amp settings and 20 percent at higher amp settings, even up to the maximum rating for the specific machine. You can find the duty cycle printed on the data plate on your MIG, arc, or TIG welder.

When you think about how you weld as a normal cycle, even for MIG welding, you will realize that you seldom weld for 10 minutes without stopping for some reason, such as to get a better position for making a good weld. For MIG welding, you may need to stop and wire brush the weld or chip slag off the weld if you are using flux core wire. And even if you are using shielding gas, you will find that if you weld for even 5 minutes on a seam, you will likely

111

HINTS FOR MIG WELDING

By the very nature of the relatively small diameter wire used for MIG welding, you always have a cold start at the beginning of your weld bead. In some cases, you will actually see a cold lap at the first of your weld, and then the weld bead smoothes out and looks good until you are at the end of the weld, especially at the edge of the part you are welding. As stated in Chapter 7, you may need to tack weld some run-off tabs to each starting and stopping part of your project. These run-off tabs will help the wire welder heat up the part for better penetration and will protect the part at the far edge from the excessive heat of the finished weld puddle.

The opposite can happen to you when you are welding thin tubing, such as a frame on a four-wheel-drive ATV or when welding a tailpipe or a muffler onto your truck's exhaust system. The cure for the cold start is to turn up the heat as much as you need to in order to create a good molten puddle at the beginning of the weld. But you risk being too hot at the first ½ inch of the weld and could burn a hole in your part. Burned holes when MIG welding are a bear to repair. You often have to stop, grind the hole, and either gas or TIG weld the hole shut. MIG welding wire will just go into the hole. So, the way to weld thin metal is to start the weld, and when you see it is too hot, let off the trigger and let the puddle cool for 2 or 3 seconds and start the weld again. Try it, it works!

A picture is worth a thousand words, but a hands-on view of a professional welder at work is worth even more. You could read this book or a college textbook many times, but if you watch a pro welding a similar project to yours, you can learn to MIG weld a lot faster and better than if you read all the books that were ever written about MIG welding. After you try to MIG weld for a few hours, stop, and drive to your local welding fab shop and ask if you can bring your helmet and protective clothes to the pro shop and watch the welder while he or she welds for an hour or two. Make sure to read about how to MIG weld first. Don't take up the welder's time until you know what to look for.

Read your operator's manual. It will save you a lot of time if you take the time to sit down and study the welding machine operator's manual before you even plug in the machine. Reading the manual can save you from damaging your brand new machine. Most of the standard brands of welding machines have a detailed operator's manual because the manufacturers have found that a new welding operator really does need to know all the tricks to correctly use their machine. You will find great tips and hints in the manual. It would be beneficial for you to sign up for an evening welding class at your local high school or community college. Even if you just visit the local trade school, you will notice that all their welding machines are heavy duty and not the lightweight cheap models. Take a hint from this and don't buy a cheap welder.

MIG WELDING, GAS, AND FLUX CORE

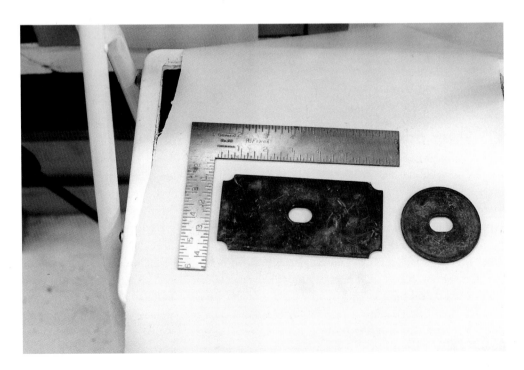

Many forms of hard facing can be used on grader and dozer blades and skip-loaders. These two hardened-steel plates were made by Cronatron Welding Systems, Inc., in Charlotte, North Carolina. They are designed to be welded around their edges and the slot in the center to attach them to the blades. The welding can be done with a wire-feed machine. This method is a lot faster than running many beads of hard-facing weld. Courtesy Cronatron Welding Systems, Inc.

This is what the guts of a heavy-duty MIG machine look like. It has a precision wire-roller gear drive with very useful adjustments and controls not found on any of the low-priced foreign-manufactured models. Quality pays off! Courtesy Miller Electric Company, Inc.

MIG WELDING, GAS, AND FLUX CORE

get a warp in the weld because you are heating the metal for too much of the seam's length.

Trailer fabricating factories are one of the most heavy duty of all farm welding operations and the welders there seldom weld for more than 3 or 4 minutes and then they stop and change positions, which allows the welding machine to cool off. With stick welding, it usually takes less than 1 minute to use up a stick of welding rod, then the welder has to stop, get another stick of rod, put it into the stinger (rod holder), and then start again. Therefore the welder usually only welds for 5 minutes out of the allowable 10 minutes and stays within the duty cycle of the welding machine.

WHAT IF YOU EXCEED THE DUTY CYCLE OF YOUR WELDING MACHINE?

There was a time in the 1960s when some of the mail order house welding machines were built with aluminum coil,

instead of copper, windings in their transformers. These cheap, lightweight welding machines had a duty cycle of about a minute. In the case of some of the arc welding machines, you would be able to notice the power (heat) at the weld puddle dropping as you were welding the very first stick of rod. Fortunately, aluminum winding welders are no longer manufactured for that reason.

If you are able to outrun your welder's duty cycle by welding steady without stopping for more minutes than the duty cycle allows, your machine will lose power similar to the aluminum winding machines. If you notice that happening, you will have to time yourself and only weld the percentage of 10 minutes that the machine is rated for at the amp setting you are using. Find something to do while the machine cools, such as chipping and wire brushing the welds or have a cup of coffee while the poor machine rests.

CHAPTER 9
SPECIAL HARD-TO-WELD METALS

ALUMINUM, CAST IRON, STAINLESS STEEL, AND SPECIAL PROCESSES

In the blacksmith's days, it would have been almost impossible to find a blacksmith shop that could weld aluminum or cast iron. If you broke one of these metal parts, you were usually out of luck. Today, there are numerous specialty welding rods and polymers that can simplify your farm and ranch life. Several of these relatively new processes are demonstrated and explained in this book. With a small amount of practice, you can easily master the special practices that will allow you to make repairs on aluminum castings, cast iron, and stainless steels, including thin sections and even "pot metal" that was the common metal for making older automobile emblems and carburetors. Most of these specialty welding rods are proprietary, which means that the company or companies that sell them likely have a patent or trademark on their products, but several are also available as generic products. This chapter will describe a few special products, and you can ask your local dealer if he has similar products. Comparing the generic products to these proprietary products is up to you.

ALUMINUM CUTTING

In the accompanying photos, the Cronacut Eagle 1100 cutting rod is being used to cut several metals, including aluminum castings, cast iron, and steel. The rod is 1/8 inch in diameter and is used with an AC and a DC straight-polarity welder. The amps were set at 150, but no air pressure was used, just the blowing force of the special rod. The rod comes in several diameters, including 3/32 inch up to 1/4 inch. The procedure is to point the electrode in the direction of the desired cut, strike an arc, and the aluminum will immediately melt and start to blow away. The resulting cut will be about double the diameter of the 1100 rod. The cut will be much faster than any other method, including using a band saw. A very positive aspect to this special cutting rod is that it can be used in the field without any gouging air pressure. When the rod is used on aluminum, metal will be made ready to arc weld in place with just a little wire brushing with a small stainless-steel brush.

This special rod will also cut cast iron, Monel, mild steel, stainless steel, and just about any metal except magnesium. The reason it won't cut magnesium is because magnesium will catch fire and continue to burn if cut at high temperature. Don't try cutting a magnesium Volkswagen Bug engine block with this rod. A fire department would not be able to put out the resulting fire.

ARC WELDING ALUMINUM CASTINGS

Arc welding aluminum was once an impossible task, but with a special arc-welding rod and pre-heating the casting to 400 degrees Fahrenheit, you can weld aluminum as easily as steel. In the photos in this chapter, a Lincoln 175-amp arc and TIG welder is set at 110 amps and DC+. The resulting arc weld was as smooth as any TIG weld. This rod can be used to build up and repair aluminum cylinder heads, cracked aluminum engine blocks, aluminum transmission

A special cutting rod is being used to cut an aluminum casting. The rod is Cronacut Eagle 1100 and is operated here by a Lincoln TIG 175-amp welding machine, set to 150 amps, on DC straight polarity.

The gap cut in the previous photo is now being welded shut with Cronaweld 510 rod. The machine is set to DC reverse polarity at 110 amps. Another brand of aluminum arc welding rod is Harris number 26. Preheating the coating to about 350 degrees Fahrenheit helps penetrate the aluminum.

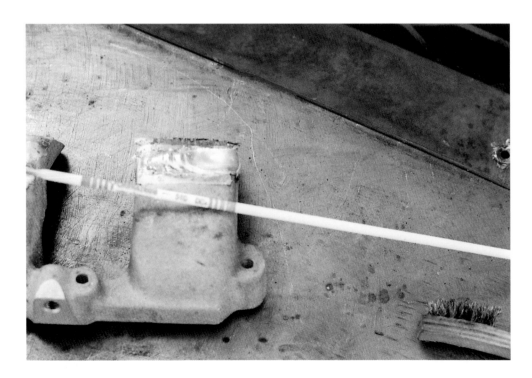

This is the weld made on an aluminum intake manifold. The heat was too high, and it should have been set about 30 amps lower. A new stick of aluminum rod is laying on the part.

This cast-iron exhaust manifold has been severed by 1/4-inch-diameter Cronacut Eagle 1100 rod with a Lincoln 175-amp machine set on DC straight polarity. An AC welder can be used, too. A smaller cut could have been made with 3/32-inch-diameter rod.

Next, the cut in the cast-iron exhaust manifold is welded using a Cronacast 211 arc welding rod, with the welding machine set to AC and 75 amps. This is a very easy weld to make.

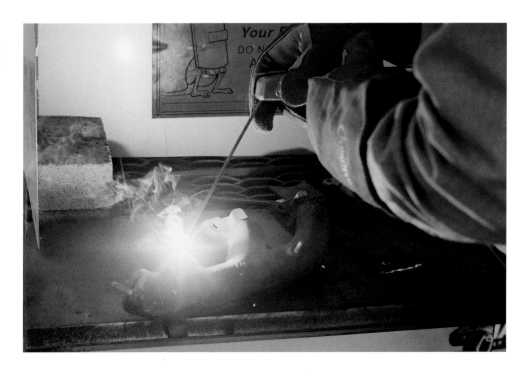

The finished product, a really nice weld on a cast-iron exhaust manifold, was made with a special Cronacast 211 welding rod. A stick of the 3/32-inch-diameter rod is lying on the manifold.

The welder is quickly piercing a ³⁄₁₆-inch-diameter hole in a piece of ¼-inch steel strap by using a ³⁄₃₂-inch-diameter number 1100 Cronacut Eagle rod. This hole took less than 3 seconds to make.

The small hole on the right was pierced in less than 5 seconds in the previous picture, but the second hole was too hot and grew because the heat was still in the steel strap from the first hole. Wait a couple of minutes before making two holes close together.

You probably don't need to weld files to mild steel, but if you do, have two unknown pieces of steel and use the Cronaweld 333 welding rod. You'll get a beautiful crack-free weld like this one.

cases, and a multitude of other farm and ranch projects. This rod is Cronaweld 510, and a ⅛-inch diameter rod was used. The rod also comes in diameters from ³⁄₃₂- to ⁵⁄₃₂-inch. Harris Company also makes a good aluminum arc-welding rod that can also be used as a flux-covered gas-welding rod. See Chapter 10 for more information.

CUTTING CAST IRON

Just as aluminum can be cut with an arc welder, cast iron can also be cut with an arc welder. This was once a dreadful task, but with the Cronacut Eagle 1100 cutting rod, it's a piece of cake to cut an exhaust flange off an old exhaust manifold or to gouge out and repair a cracked manifold. The same process holds true for repairing cracked engine blocks, plowshare clamps, and any cast-iron part. You should practice on an old piece of cast iron before you try this new rod. It cuts so fast that it could get ahead of you if you're not familiar with its capabilities. The rod will operate with a buzzbox AC welder, an AC/DC welder with DC straight polarity, or any farm welding stick machine.

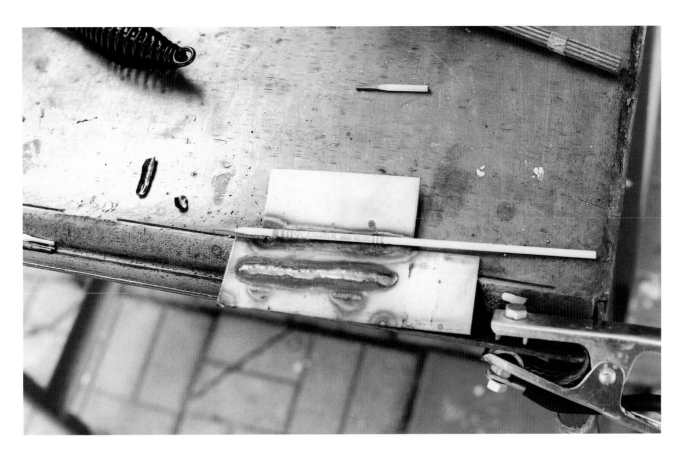

This beautiful arc weld on a piece of 0.090-inch stainless-steel sheet shows the kind of weld you can expect with a Cronaweld Eagle 3880 rod in an AC machine set to 75 amps. Stainless rod can also be used on rusty, dirty steel with good results.

ARC WELDING CAST IRON

Not too many years ago, the only way to effectively weld cast iron was to preheat it to about 350 degrees Fahrenheit, use Ni-Rod, and repeatedly peen it. Often the weld would crack anyway. In the years after World War II, many old farm tractors had been left to sit during the winter with radiator water in the engine block. Of course, the engine froze and the cast-iron water jackets burst or cracked. Many were sent to the scrap yard because the blocks had cracked and no one could weld them properly. Now that problem has been solved.

A high-tech cast-iron welding rod is available that will permanently fix broken cast iron. Cronacast 211 rod can be used on welders with AC or DC reverse polarity. It has a tensile strength of up to 84,000 psi and can be easily machined, unlike the old Ni-Rod that always became hard and brittle. When the new 211 rod is used, it looks a lot like chrome and is smooth, not grainy. Practice on an old piece of cast iron to get the hang of using the rod on cast iron. And be sure to take time to read the manufacturer's instructions before beginning the cast-iron weld repair.

DRILLING/PIERCING HOLES IN STEEL

To line up or create new holes in steel (or any other metal) you'll need a stick of Cronatron 1100. If you need to drill a hole out in the field or in the shop but your drills are too dull to do the job quickly, the Cronatron 1100 can make any hole from the rod diameter to as large as you want. Just turn up the welding machine and hold the rod as you would a drill, and within a second or two, a hole will be pierced into the metal.

UNSURE OF THE STEELS TO BE JOINED?

With Cronaweld 333 rod, you can weld a tool-steel-hardened hand file to a piece of mild-steel angle or anything that a magnet will stick to. Once the weld is cooled, you can just tap the slag cover, and the weld will appear as clean and pretty as if it were chrome. This rod works so well on so many things that you'll find yourself using it for almost all farm repairs. It is strong at 125,000-psi tensile strength, but it isn't brittle when welded. It has an elongation of 35 percent for shock and crack resistance. It will even weld leaf springs without cracking the spring. It can also be used

The bent paper clip in this picture was soldered with the propane lighter shown here. The tensile strength of the solder is 22,000 psi. The heat required to solder is 425 degrees Fahrenheit.

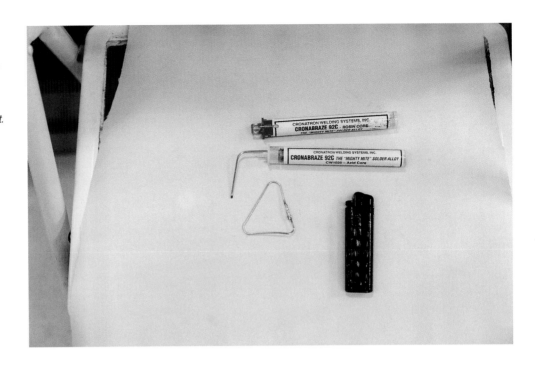

Yes, there is such a thing as a "cold" weld, and JB Weld is a very good product for this, but it can take several hours to set up. The long stick is a Cronatron Poly-Quick Stick, and it's used for making repairs that need to set up quickly or are wet.

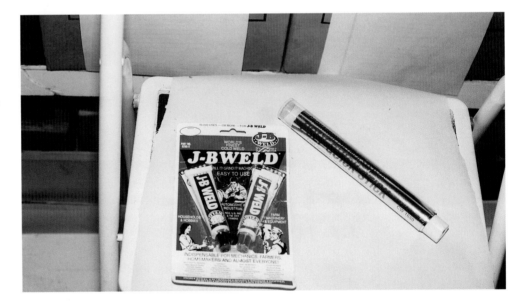

to build up worn shafts. Cronaweld 333 rod is truly unique, and it works miracles for broken studs or bolt extraction. See page 42 for directions on how to use it to remove broken studs.

ARC WELDING STAINLESS-STEEL TANKS, POTS, AND PIPES

Cronatron makes a very high quality stainless-steel welding rod for arc welding, but it's best to have a few sizes of Cronaweld Eagle 3880 stick rod in your stock of welding supplies. This rod can look better than a perfect TIG weld if

you take your time and let the slag cool for a few minutes before chipping it off. The slag will peel off itself if the weld is done well. The weld will come out looking like chrome and will be sound at up to 90,000-psi tensile strength.

HIGH-STRENGTH LOW-TEMP SOLDER

Solder is not just for cold water buckets. A solder can hold 22,000 pounds per square inch and only needs 425 degrees Fahrenheit to melt. It melts at such a low temperature that a cigarette lighter will do some of the smaller soldering jobs, but avoid touching the flux with the flame because the flux

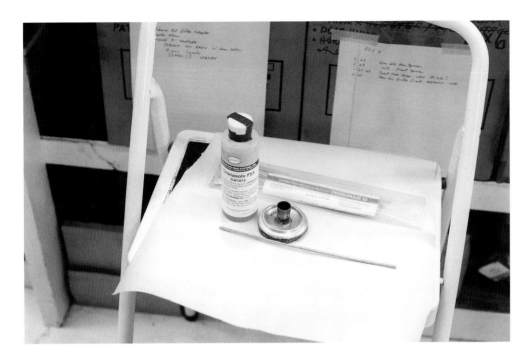

Cronasolv F53 flux was used with number 53 solder to attach this piece of copper tubing to the aluminum can. This solder and flux is great for soldering any combination of metals, including aluminum, copper, brass, and pot metals.

Poly-Quick Stick makes strong repairs, as is demonstrated by this steel bolt molded into threads on the coffee-can lid.

can be burned or charred by direct flame. Buy Cronabraze 92C in either rosin core or acid core. Rosin core works well for wiring, where you can't rinse it off after soldering. If you are able to rinse the part in water after soldering, then acid core works the best.

MORE HIGH-STRENGTH MULTI-METAL SOLDER

Has anybody ever said to you that you can't weld copper to aluminum to stainless steel or to brass, or weld pot metal? Cronatron makes a lead-type soldering alloy that will weld hood ornaments on collectors' cars, and will solder copper-tubing fittings to the newer aluminum refrigeration units. It has a tensile strength of 17,500 psi and a melting point of only 360 degrees Fahrenheit. A good soldering iron will work with this metal joiner. It must have a separate honey-like liquid flux to make it stick. Do not use a direct flame to heat it because the liquid flux will char or burn. The trade name is Cronabraze 53, and it requires Cronasolv F53 flux to activate it.

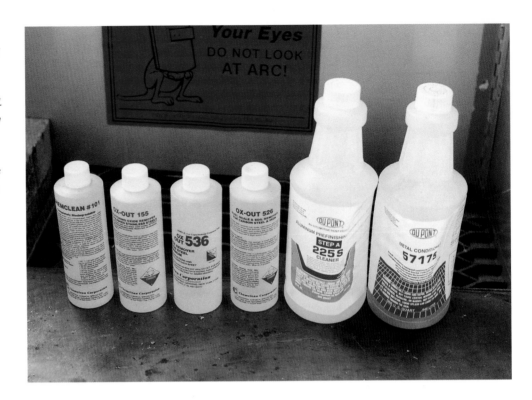

Left to right: Biodegradable Chemclean 101 is for degreasing metals. Ox-Out 155 is a non-etching product for cleaning welds off polished stainless steel. Ox-Out 536 removes oxides from stainless and aluminum. Ox-Out 526 is a scale and soil remover for steel and iron, and it contains phosphoric acid. DuPont 225S is used for etching and cleaning aluminum. DuPont 5717S is a phosphoric acid-based rust remover for steels and irons.

VARIOUS FLUXES

The fluxes discussed in this section make all the difference in blacksmithing and modern weld shops. Solar Flux has been around for many years, and it's rumored that the company was originally formed to develop a solution for Charles Lindberg's airplane, *Spirit of St. Louis,* for his epic flight to Paris, France. They needed a way to fusion weld the stainless-steel firewall for the flight, and no previous method had been developed. Solar Flux will work to protect the weld on all types of stainless-steel welding, including arc/stick welding, but especially for gas welding. Just follow the directions on mixing the powder with alcohol to form a protective paste over the weld bead and the backside of the weld.

Aluminum flux will come in handy for oxy-acetylene fusion welding aluminum, and brazing fluxes are necessary for steel and cast-iron brazing repairs. Several of the silver brazing alloys require a special type of flux to clean the metal while silver brazing.

COLD WELDING?

There will be times when you don't want to heat the part, such as when there is oil or gasoline in a tank, but the tank has a leak. The long-term fix in cases like that is to use JB Weld, an epoxy glue mixed with steel filings for superior strength. JB Weld is useful where the part can be cleaned and set upright for about 24 hours. It will run like paint if it isn't supported in a flat position. It is always stronger to put a patch on the repair to support the JB Weld. Cronatron also makes a Poly-Quick Stick for repairing parts, even under water. The repair is as strong as a pot-metal casting would be at 6,000-psi tensile strength. Just cut off a piece, peel the paper off, knead it until it's mixed, and then you can hand-form or towel it into place for the repair.

WELD CLEANING LIQUIDS

The DuPont chemical company's slogan "better living through chemistry" is still true. We have a number of miracle liquids that will eat rust, dissolve aluminum corrosion, remove heat stains from stainless steel, and generally prepare metals before and after welding. The appendix lists addresses for suppliers of these handy products. You can become the local welding expert when you use these special chemicals to help in your metal preparations prior to welding.

OTHER METAL JOINING PRODUCTS

It's almost safe to say that if it's metal, somebody has a method of repairing and joining it in new fabrication. But don't get bilked by the state fair hucksters that can show you how to weld almost anything. They are probably hawking a version of the Cronatron 53, which you already know about, at a highly marked up price. Don't fall for their scam. And besides, who really has the need to weld beer cans together anyway?

CHAPTER 10
WHERE TO BUY WELDING SUPPLIES

LOCAL WELDING SUPPLY STORES

It's easy to stop by the local welding supply store to buy extra welding rods, exchange a couple of gas cylinders, and look over some of the specialty items that may have come in since you stopped by the last time. That's one way to stay up-to-date with the latest in welding technology. With farmers now depending on GPS (global positioning system) technology to plant straight rows and using computers to decide which

crops to plant and to help with the bookkeeping, it makes sense to depend on the latest in electronics to help with maintenance welding around the farm. You'll likely want to update some of your equipment to improve your next welding project.

Another helpful thing about local welding supply dealers is the occasional welding product show. A typical tent sale usually includes a hot dog and hamburger meal plus coffee,

This building houses a local pipe and steel company near White Sands National Monument in New Mexico. Pueblo Pipe and Steel can cut short lengths of pipe or steel, and they also sell full 20-foot lengths.

Here's a stock of expanded metal, steel angle, rods, steel strap, bar stock, and channel of almost any size your project needs. Just check your yellow pages for companies like Pueblo Pipe and Steel.

doughnuts, and cold drinks. While you're at the show, you can eat, drink, and take time to check out the latest and best new products. A welding supply dealer may well have factory reps from four or more companies on hand to demonstrate new products and answer questions.

While you're there, take your time and do some shopping to find some helpful products for your shop. Things like soapstone marking pencils, welder's caps to keep sparks out of your hair, new welding gloves, books on the newest welding methods, and other useful welding supplies would be excellent additions to your shop.

LOCAL STEEL SUPPLY STORES

If you plan to build some specialty wagons, animal pens, loading racks, or other things to help make life easier, you'll surely enjoy going shopping at a local steel, iron, and pipe supply store. You may even find some steel shapes that you didn't know existed. A sheet of expanded metal will usually come in handy for future projects, as will a sheet of diamond-plate aluminum. Steel supply stores usually have specialty items such as fence finials (decorative tips) for steel posts and gates. When you go to the store, take your lumber rack or flatbed truck, because most steel products come in 20-foot sections that won't fit in an 8-foot pickup bed.

LOCAL CHAIN STORES

Chain stores such as Tractor Supply Company; Harbor Freight; Lowe's; Home Depot; Sears, Roebuck and Co.; and many auto parts stores also carry welding supplies. If you need welding rod or a new gas welder, you can likely find it at one of the major chain stores. Some chain stores even sell large engine-driven generators and welding machines.

In this very complete stock of steel products at Pueblo Pipe and Steel near Alamogordo, New Mexico, you can find square, rectangular, and round tubing, plus several sizes of I-beams, channels, and large round stock.

In the back room at Pueblo Pipe and Steel, several sizes of steel channel and round tubing are in stock. This ought to give you some ideas about what you want to use in your next project.

These ready-made fencepost decorations should give you some ideas about what design you'd like to have for the fence around your house or for your front gate at the farm.

Here are some other decorative fence-post items that are ready to weld to a fence. There are also some cast-aluminum decorations that could be used on fences.

A car roof rack could haul under 500 pounds of steel from the supplier to your shop in a pinch; check your rack's weight capacity to be sure. But a ladder rack on the bed of your pickup would be better and could haul more weight.

You could hook one of these new machines onto the hitch of your pickup and tow it home and start welding today.

SPECIALTY SHOPS

In some areas, you'll find specialty shops advertised in the yellow pages under the categories "Machines, Farm and Ranch" and "Supply, Equipment." It pays to check out all these stores to make sure that you're fully up-to-date about the welding equipment and supplies that are available to you.

MAIL ORDER WELDING SUPPLIES

The old adage of "needing a part on Saturday morning" is something that you need to consider when ordering from a catalog. If you decide to buy a welding machine that was manufactured in a foreign country, you need to find out if that company can sell you an emergency repair part on a Saturday morning. It's most likely that you'll have to wait for replacement parts, even if they actually sell replacement parts. Just finding a person who will take your order may be difficult. What if you decide to convert your MIG welder to an SMAW welder? Does the company have a telephone number and a parts catalog? If not, don't buy the welding machine!

But there are some very dependable welding supply companies that sell only by catalog, phone, or fax orders. These companies provide some specialty products that do a great job and are not available at any local welding store. Veteran farmers remember the traveling salesmen who once stopped by to sell products that were an absolute necessity for making a living. There are still a few route salesmen who can call on you at home.

WELDING ROD

Welding rod comes in grades, just like nuts and bolts. That's right—you can buy cheap-quality welding rod or you can buy high-quality, certified welding rod. What's the difference?

You can find welding businesses listed in the yellow pages, such as Valley Welders Supply Co. This local welding supply sells welding gases, Lincoln welders, Miller welders, and most necessary welding supplies including parts for welding machines.

Don West Jr. shows a large assortment of welding gas cylinders that are full and ready to sell to customers. Don works for Valley Welders Supply in Alamogordo, New Mexico. At the left are a large number of medical oxygen cylinders for the local hospital.

Don West Jr. points to the numbers on a cylinder that show when the last hydro test was done. This cylinder was tested in March of 2000 and is good for 10 years. You might find a set of numbers that shows 7*38, which is July 1938. But you will also find at least 7 more sets of numbers that indicate the cylinder has been hydro tested at least 7 times, once every 10 years. Don't buy a cylinder that is almost ready for a hydro test.

Here's an example: Airplane builders typically spend $100,000 to build a fast, high-tech airplane. Then they spend $75,000 to purchase a new aircraft engine and propeller for the plane. Does it make economic sense to spend less than $5 for the welding rod that holds the plane's engine mount together?

You can go to your local welding supply store and buy one pound of no-name copper-coated steel welding rod for as little as $1.50. The welding supply store has no idea what the rod is made of, except that a magnet will stick to it, so it must be steel, not solid copper, aluminum, or stainless steel. It is also a fact that the cheap copper-coated steel welding rod is usually made from scrap metal—old cars, old bicycle frames, old tractor parts, and old concrete reinforcing bars salvaged for scrap. Not the kind of metal you'd want to hold an airplane engine mount together, or to hold the front suspension together on a farm tractor.

But even if you want to weld an engine mount to hold a $2,000 engine in a $10,000 airplane, $40 for the welding rod versus $1.50 for the cheap rod is not a high price to pay. Your own safety and well-being is surely worth the few extra dollars for the good welding rod.

RESULTS WITH CHEAP ROD

If cheap, reclaimed scrap welding rod is used to TIG or MIG weld 4130 steel, you can expect a number of defects

Don West Sr. of Valley Welding Supply shows a pair of small cylinders for the gas-welding set shown in this chapter. The small cylinder holds 10 cubic feet of acetylene and costs $12.34 to refill. The larger green cylinder holds 21 cubic feet of oxygen and costs $9.63 to refill. There is also a hazardous material charge of $7.00 for the acetylene cylinder. The oxygen cylinder can be refilled on the spot, but the acetylene cylinder must be exchanged because of the much longer filling time required for acetylene.

A tent sale at a local welding supply store. The Hobart factory rep drives around his territory and demonstrates his company's welding and cutting machines. He'd be happy to take your order for a brand-new welding machine.

The power tool counter at a local Sears store, with numerous types of air compressors for any shop. The largest compressor you can fit in your shop would be the best choice.

The welding equipment counter at a local Sears store. Note the spare parts for welders that the store sells. This is a sign of good service.

The local Sears store sells this lightweight 100-volt arc welding machine. Be aware that this machine will only weld 1/8-inch and thinner steel.

A load of scrap metal bound for a furnace to be melted into cheap welding rod. Who knows what the metal is? You should always buy quality welding rod for your quality farm projects, not just any mystery metal.

in your welds. Cheap welding rod will bubble and boil and leave big holes of porosity in your welds because the cheap stuff has unknown foreign matter in it, including large amounts of dirt, slag, grease, and moisture.

The copper coating on cheap rod does not mix with steel, and it enters the weld puddle to cause defects such as crater cracking and hydrogen embrittlement from exposure to moisture trapped between the flaking copper and the cracks and crevices in the cheap rod.

COPPER-COATED ROD

In many places in this book, you've been advised to use copper as a tungsten arc starting block and to use copper strips as backup strips when welding thin sheets of steel, aluminum, and stainless steel.

Copper is used because it will not mix or fuse with steel or other metals. When used for a heat-sink backup strip, copper won't stick to the welded seam.

If you cut a cross-section out of a common piece of copper-coated steel welding rod and magnify it 3,000 times, you will be able to see that the copper coating is not adhering to the rod, but flaking off. The copper coating is not a part of the rod.

Then why do manufacturers use copper to coat steel welding rod? Copper-coated steel rod will rust, so the copper isn't used as a rust preventative. Manufacturers coat steel welding rod with copper to help make the wire drawing/sizing dies last longer. Copper is used to lubricate the drawing dies. Manufacturers also use soaps and oils that become embedded in the wire as it is drawn through the dies to size it.

The only thing small about this gas welding rig is the size of the cylinders at 10 and 21 cubic feet, respectively. The welding rig was purchased at a local Home Depot for $279. Within an hour, the tanks had been filled and exchanged, and the torch was cutting 1-inch-thick steel plate, but not for very long, because the tanks don't hold much gas.

Go to the hardware store and buy some 10-foot lengths of plastic pipe and caps to make some waterproof welding-rod holders, as shown here. You can also buy arc welding rod holders like those you see here. Courtesy Cronatron Welding Systems, Inc.

NUTS AND BOLTS

At the beginning of this chapter, the grades of welding rod were related to the various grades of nuts and bolts. You're probably aware of the no-markings bolts that you can buy at the hardware store. These bolts are made from steel of unknown origin, and they can twist and break very easily, so you don't want to use them for anything but lawn furniture. The next higher-quality bolt grade, SAE 5, is commonly used to hold bumpers and fenders on cars. Moving up in quality are bolts commonly used to attach cylinder heads to car engines. They have six marks on their heads, and they're SAE grade 8. Approximately equal in strength to SAE grade-8 bolts are AN bolts, specified for use in missiles and certified aircraft.

It's obvious that low-grade hardware-store bolts are cheaper than grade-8 and AN bolts, but quality nuts and bolts are more than worth the extra cost in safety-critical systems, such as aircraft and race cars. As with welding rod, never use the cheap stuff. Someone's life may depend on it.

EXPENSIVE COMMERCIAL GRADE

A number of welding supply firms offer excellent welding rod and supplies. But be aware that, although a firm's name is on the packaging, that firm may not have manufactured the materials in question. Many firms contract with manufacturers to make welding rod and supplies and package them under their proprietary names. Except for the MSD sheets required by OSHA, these firms don't tell customers the exact metal and material content in their products. This practice is common in the welding supply industry. If you ask for certification sheets and can't get them, it is because

MC-grade welding wire. This desiccant packaged 6 1/4-pound bag of vacuum-melt, metallurgically controlled welding wire from United States Welding Corporation is by far the best kind of welding rod to use on TIG welds.

another manufacturer makes the supplies and the second company repackages the product.

However, the fact that you pay $200 for five pounds of welding rod does not guarantee a better product. For instance, one particular repackaging company sells a little wire tip cleaner for gas torches for $45; a local welding supply store sells the same wire tip cleaner for $4.50! It pays to shop for price and quality.

WELDING GASES

At this time, you can obtain compressed gases for welding (including acetylene, oxygen, hydrogen, argon, helium, CO_2, and combination mixed gases) in a number of ways. Suppliers in different geographic regions vary in how they sell consumable gases.

One welding gas retail dealer may only lease gas bottles. This means that you pay a $125 deposit on each gas bottle and a $10 monthly lease fee as long as you keep the bottle. You also pay $25 for the argon gas in the bottle. In one year, this dealer will get $270 from you for each bottle of gas you lease from him.

Just across town, another welding gas retailer may sell you the same size bottle for $125, give you the first fill of argon free, with no monthly rent on the bottle, because you bought it. You can keep the bottle for a year and sell it to a friend or back to the dealer. So you saved $145 the first year on each bottle you bought rather than leased. As has been said before, shop around before you buy.

BOTTLE SIZES

Don't make the mistake of buying or leasing the very largest or the very smallest gas bottles, even if you're operating a full-time welding fabrication shop. The largest bottles will be a nuisance to handle and the smallest ones go empty far too quickly. See page 142 for bottle sizes.

FLUXES

In researching10 flux supplier catalogs, I discovered that no company will tell the consumer what the chemicals it puts in its products that make them do the special protecting and cleaning jobs that each brand is advertised to do. And if you attempted to buy one of every part number, you would be really confused because 10 manufacturers make more than 100 different products.

COMPANIES THAT PRODUCE FLUX

Superior Flux and Manufacturing Company
6615 Park Boulevard
Cleveland, OH 44143
Phone: (440) 348-3000
Fax: (440) 349-3003

Bradford Derustit Corporation
P.O. Box 280
Tualatin, OR 97062
Phone: (877) 899-5315
Fax: (877) 285-2080
Stainless Steel Flux
(Solar Flux)
Golden Empire Corporation
P.O. Box 2129
Morehead City, NC 28557
Phone: 1-252-808-3511
Fax: 1-252-808-3711

For special jobs, contact one of these manufacturers or your local welding supply retailer to find specific fluxes for specific methods and preferred joining methods.

OTHER WELDING SUPPLY COMPANIES REFERENCED IN THIS BOOK

Aircraft Spruce and Specialty Company
P.O. Box 4000
Corona, CA 92878-4000
Phone: (951) 372-9555
Fax: (951) 372-0555

Cronatron Welding Systems Inc.
6510 Northpark Boulevard
Charlotte, NC 28216-2367
Phone: (800) 526-3899

ESAB Welding & Cutting Products
411 South Ebenezer Road
P.O. Box 100545
Florence, SC 29501-7916
Phone: (843) 669-4411
Fax: (843) 664-4258

Harris Welco
P.O. Box 69, 1051 York Road
Kings Mountain, NC 28086
Phone: (513) 754-2000

Lancaster Alloys Company
42328 10th Street West
Lancaster, CA 93534
Phone: (800) LA-WIRES, (661) 723-1397
Fax: (661) 723-1580

Lincoln Electric Company
22801 St. Clair Avenue
Cleveland, OH 44117
Phone: (216) 481-8100
Fax: (216) 486-1751

United States Welding Corporation
3579 Highway 50 East Suite #104
Carson City, NV 89701-2826
Phone: (800) 423-5964 (755) 883-7878
Fax: (775) 883-7776

Chemical Cleaning Products

Chemclean Corporation
130/45 180th St.
Springfield Garden, NY 11434
Phone: 1-718-525-4500
Fax: 1-718-481-6470

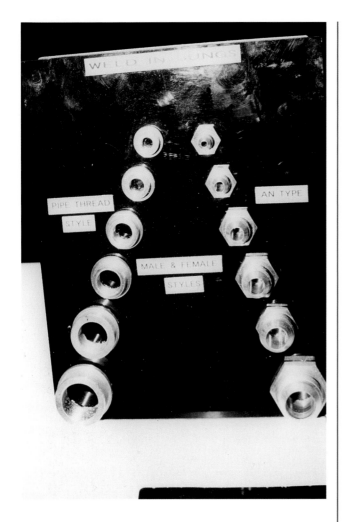

Weld-on fittings like the assortment shown here make an easy job of finishing aluminum oil tanks, fuel tanks, and water-recovery tanks. Buy an assortment of these fittings to have on hand for special welding projects.

Gas Welding Equipment and Parts

Harris Calorific Division
2345 Murphy Blvd.
Gainesville, GA 30504
Phone: 1-800-241-0804
Fax: 1-770-535-0544
www.harriscal.com

Victor Thermadyne
P.O. Box 1007
Denton, TX 76202-1007
Phone: 1-800-426-1888
Fax: 1-800-535-0557

Welding Machines and Parts

Hobart Welding Machines
See Miller Electric Corporation

Lincoln Electric Company
22801 St. Clair Ave.
Cleveland, OH 44117-1199
Phone: 1-216-481-8100
www.lincolnelectric.com

Miller Electric Manufacturing Co.
1635 W. Spencer St.
PO Box 1079
Appleton, WI 54912
1-800-426-4553
www.millerwelds.com

Welding Rod and Supplies

Cronatron Welding Systems, Inc.
6510 Northpark Blvd.
Charlotte, NC 28216-2367
Phone: 1-704-598-1225
Fax: 1-704-598-7572
www.cronatronwelding.com

SOURCES FOR METALS

You may already have a favorite place where you buy 4130 steel tubing, 6061 aluminum, and 308 and 316 stainless steel. If you're buying them from a local dealer, it's a good idea to check around to make sure that you're getting certified materials and that you're paying a fair price.

Listed below in alphabetical order are a number of companies that sell retail quantities of aluminum, steel, and various other metals that you may need for your performance welding projects.

Metals Suppliers
A B C Metals & Supply Co.
2931 Ventura Boulevard
Oxnard, CA 93031
Phone: 805-485-7805
Fax: 805-981-0394
Aircraft Spruce and Specialty Company East
452 Dividend Drive
Peachtree City, GA 302
Phone: (770) 487-2310
1-800-831-2949
Fax: (770) 487-2308

Aircraft Spruce Europe
9 Cam Center, Wilbury WY
Hitchin, Hertfordshire England SG4 0TW
Phone: 44-1462-441995
Fax: 44-1462-442228

Aircraft Spruce and Specialty Company West
225 Airport Circle
Corona, CA 92880
Phone: (909) 372-9555
Customer Service: 800-861-3192
Fax: 909-372-0555

Aircraft Steel
923 Country Road 7
Erie, CO 80516-7907
Phone: 303-665-5817

CSC Racing Products Inc.
125A Harry Walker Parkway
Newmarket, Ontario
Canada L3Y7B3
Phone: (905) 954-0520

The Dillsburg Aeroplane Works
114 Saw Mill Road
Dillsburg, PA 17019-9517
Phone: (717) 432-4589

Industrial Metal Supply Co.
8300 N. San Fernando Road
Sun Valley, CA 91352-3222
Phone: (818) 729-3333
Fax: (818) 729-3334
Ventura Steel, Inc.
1885 N. Ventura Avenue
Ventura, CA 93001
Phone: 805-643-6662
Phone: 800-235-0099
Fax: 805-643-6667

Wag-Aero Group
P.O. Box 181
Lyons, WI 53148
Phone: 800-558-6868

Wicks Aircraft Supply
410 Pine Street
Highland, IL 62249
Phone: 618-654-7447
Phone: 800-221-9425
Fax: 618-654-6253

Contact information for the companies listed above was valid at time of publication.

You may also refer to your local telephone directory under the headings "Steel Products" and "Metals" for companies that sell aircraft-quality metals.

SHOPPING BY PHONE

Even if you don't live near one of the metals supply companies listed in this chapter, you can order steel, aluminum, and stainless steel over the telephone. Most metals companies do a lot of their business by shipping orders by rail and by United Parcel Service. Shipping fees are usually 2 to 5 percent of the total order cost.

If the metal tubing you order measures more than 8 feet long, it cannot be shipped by UPS, but most truck lines will

MIL-SPECS FLUXES

Solar Flux (1 pound containers)
Type 1
For nickel, Inconel, etc. Mix with methanol to form a thick paste. Works well to clean and protect the backside of gas, TIG, and MIG welds.

Solar Flux (1 pound containers)
Type B
For all stainless steels. Mix with methanol to form a thick paste. Apply to backside of gas, MIG, and TIG welds to ensure sugar-free welds.

Solar Flux (1 pound containers)
Type 202
For all gas welds on aluminum. Works well with TIG or MIG also. Makes gas welding aluminum easy.

No. 65 Flux
Flux for welding and soldering all metals except aluminum and magnesium. For air conditioners, refrigeration, stainless. 200 to 600 degrees Fahrenheit.

deliver it to your door, even in residential areas. Once or twice in many years of ordering tubing, I've encountered truck lines that want the shipment picked up at their dock, but truck drivers are usually happy to deliver to my shop door.

CATALOGS

Every metals supply company listed in this appendix can supply you with a catalog. In several catalogs, extra information is presented, such as inner diameter, outer diameter, strength of materials, common manufacturing practices, and other pertinent information. Some of the catalogs are free, and others are offered at a nominal cost with a refundable coupon for the first purchase.

RECOMMENDED SUPPLIES

The remainder of this chapter is divided into sections of recommended welding supplies for MIG, and gas welding. Finally, there's a section on general welding supplies.

Within a few days, the 4130 steel tubing that is being unpacked in this photo was cut, fitted, and welded into an assembly.

MIG WIRE CHANGES

MIG wire uses the same chemical mix of alloys as is used in TIG welding the same application. One current problem with MIG wire selection is that every significant company in the business is continuing to experiment with metallurgy to improve weldability of MIG wires. It would be wise to talk to a factory representative about your specific MIG welding requirements before investing in significant amounts of MIG welding wire.

DO OR DON'T: FLUX OR 4130 STEEL?

Gas welding (OFW), oxygen-acetylene welding of 4130 steel, does not require any flux, and in fact attempting to use flux on the top side of the weld will make welding very difficult. However, it will aid the welding if a Solar Flux paste is applied to the backside of the weld to aid in heat control on thin sheet-metal butt welds. One difficulty in using flux on 4130 is the requirement that it be removed completely before welding the backside. For the average 4130 tubular structure, no flux should be used.

SUGGESTED WELDING ROD FOR OXYACETYLENE STEEL

Oxweld Stock No. 32CMS	for 4130 Steel	(Oxweld: ESAB, South Carolina)
USW Stock No. 6457V	for 4130 Steel	(USW: United States Welding Corporation, Nevada)
AS Stock No. RG-60	for 4130 Steel	(AS: All-State, ESAB, Maryland)

SUGGESTED WELDING ROD FOR GAS WELDING ALUMINUM

CWS Stock No. CW1016†	35,000 psi	for 6061 Aluminum	CWS: Cronatron Welding Systems, North Carolina
CWS Stock No. CW1857†	34,500 psi	for 5052 Aluminum	
Welco Stock No. COR-AL†	30,000 psi	for 5052 Aluminum	Welco: Thermacote—Welco Corporation, Michigan
USW Stock No. 1374C	5 Mg	for 5052 Aluminum	USW: United States Welding Corporation, Nevada

†These aluminum rods are brazing rods, but the 30,000 to 35,000 psi tensile strength should be adequate for most fusion welding of aluminum.

SUGGESTED WELD ROD FOR GAS WELDING STAINLESS STEEL

CWS Stock No. CW1023	No. 95 Bare 95,000	TIG or Gas	(CWS: Cronatron Welding Systems, North Carolina)

SUGGESTED BRAZING RODS FOR GAS BRAZING MILD STEEL AND STAINLESS STEEL

*CWS Stock No. CW1002 No. 23F	Blue Coating	66,000	1,400–1,600°F
CWS Stock No. CW1836 No. 30F	Pink Coating	100,000	1,300–1,600°F
CWS Stock No. CW1025 No. 40F	Orange Coating (High Sivv.)	85,000	1,100°F
CWS Stock No. CW1024 No. 43F	Blue Coating	88,000	1,100°F
CWS Stock No. CW1017 No. 53	No Coating (All)	17,500	360°F

*CWS: Cronatron Welding Systems, North Carolina

Note: No. 23F and No. 30F are for most regular steel and light cast-iron brazing (economical). No. 40F is a high-priced but excellent high silver content silver brazing material that's great for stainless steel. No. 43F is a good, lower-cost silver content brazing rod for steel, copper, brass, and stainless steel.

FLUX-CORE ALUMINUM BRAZING ROD

Flux-core aluminum brazing rod is relatively new to the gas-welding field. When you use it to braze an oil tank made of 5052 aluminum, it is so close to the base metal tensile strength of 36,000 to 41,000 psi that it will give you welds as strong as fusion-welded aluminum. Actually the lowest tensile strength of 5052-O (soft) aluminum is only 29,000 psi. All of the flux-cored aluminum brazing rod listed in the previous table is above 30,000-psi tensile strength. The melting point of these flux-cored brazing rod is 1,050° to 1,100° Fahrenheit, just over 100° Fahrenheit lower than the 1,217° Fahrenheit melting point of the base metal, a difference that is not really controllable with a hand-operated oxyacetylene torch. Generally, you will end up with a good fused weld/braze joint anyway.

As in gas welding stainless steel, try to make each seam a 90-degree folded joint so that most of the heat is applied to the fold and not the flat base metal.

GENERAL-PURPOSE SOLDER

Cronantron No. 53 is a very low-temperature solder that melts at only 360 degrees Fahrenheit. And it will join all metals—aluminum to steel, copper, brass, stainless steel, etc.—with a 17,500-psi tensile strength. This would be handy in unusual metal-joining situations. It requires a honey-consistency flux to work.

METAL CLEANERS

Derustit SS-3
Stainless-steel cleaner. Cleans heat scale off stainless-steel welds.

Bradford No. 1
Metal cleaner. Cleans steel, copper, brass. Rust oxide remover.

BACKUP PASTES FOR WELD PROTECTION AND JIGGING

HTP Stock No. 12084 Heat Sponge, Ceramic Heat Sink
CWS Stock No. CW1082A Plio Jig, Ceramic Heat Sink

Check with your local welding supply retailer for 1- and 5-pound plastic cans of a moist, clay-like ceramic paste that will insulate your welds. These products work like putting a water-soaked rag by the weld to insulate the heat from the parts you don't want to overheat.

HIGH-PRESSURE CYLINDER SIZES

Oxygen, Argon, Helium, etc.

Cubic Feet	Outer Diameter	Height	Weight	Service Pressure
20	5.27"	14"	10 lbs.	2015 psi
40	7.0"	18"	23 lbs.	2015 psi
55	7.0"	23"	30 lbs.	2015 psi
80	7.0"	33"	42 lbs.	2015 psi
110	7.0"	43"	55 lbs.	2015 psi
125	7.0"	43"	55 lbs.	2265 psi
150	7.0"	46"	59 lbs.	2015 psi
220	9.0"	51"	114 lbs.	2015 psi
250	9.0"	51"	115 lbs.	2265 psi
300	9.27"	55"	135 lbs.	2400 psi
400	10.50"	66"	190 lbs.	2400 psi

LOW-PRESSURE CYLINDER SIZES, ACETYLENE

Number	Cubic Feet	Outer Dia.	Height	Weight	Service Pressure
S-10	10	4.0"	13"	7.5 lbs.	250 psi
S-40	40	6.0"	19"	23.4 lbs.	250 psi
S-75	75	7.0"	26"	43.8 lbs.	250 psi
S-145	145	8.0"	34"	74.1 lbs.	250 psi
W210	210	10.0"	32"	100.7 lbs.	250 psi

RECOMMENDED GASES FOR WELDING

Welding Process	Suggested Gases
TIG Aluminum	Argon
TIG 4130 Steel	Argon
TIG Stainless Steel	Argon
TIG Titanium	Argon
MIG Aluminum	Argon
MIG 4130 Steel	75/25% Argon and Helium
MIG Stainless Steel	Argon + 1% Oxygen
OFW Aluminum	Oxygen and Acetylene or Hydrogen
OFW 4130 Steel	Oxygen and Acetylene
Inert Gas Purging	Argon

Be sure to ask your welding gas supply dealer to describe any special gas mixtures to aid your MIG welding needs. Certain companies offer gold mix, which is 70 percent argon, 12 percent helium, and 18 percent special mix, or other unusual percentages. The dealer's experience tells them that even as little as 1 percent oxygen can greatly improve certain welding processes.

INDEX

Acetylene 134, 141
  Pressures, 61
  Regulator, 56
  Tanks, 56
Acids, storing, 31
Advanced welding, 87, 88
Air compressor, 22, 130
Air pressure gauge, 62
Air-assisted heating, 11
Allen computer tune-up test machine, 24
Alloy steel, 9
Aluminum, 34
  Buying, 47
  Cutting, 114
  Flux, 122
Arc welding (SMAW), 37, 38, 43, 81–102
  Aluminum castings, 114, 118
  Cast iron, 92, 96, 119
  Clothing for, 86
  Cutting metals, 96
  Hints, 101
  Process, 38
  Stainless steel tanks, pots, and pipes, 120
Argon, 134, 141

Band saw, 21, 24
Barns, types, 15–19
Bench grinder, 22
Bench vise, 21
Bessemer, Henry, 9
Blacksmith shops, 11, 12
Bolt removal, 42
Brass, 34
Brazing procedure, 74, 75
Bronze Age, 7

Carbon steel, 9
Carburizing flame, 70
Cast iron, 34
  Cutting, 118
Catalogs, shopping by, 138
Chain stores, 124, 127
Cleaning liquids, 122
  Biodegradable Chemclean 101, 122
  DuPont 225S, 122
  DuPont 5717S, 122
  Ox-Out 155, 122
  Ox-Out 526, 122
  Ox-Out 536, 122
CO_2, 134

Cold welding, 122
Craftsman tools, 24
Cronatron Welding Systems, Inc., 26
Cronabraze 53, 121
Cronazolv F53 flux, 121
Cut-off wheel/saw, 20, 22, 24, 45, 87
Cutting and heating, tips, 60
Cylinders, 128, 129, 135, 141

Drill press, 24
Duty cycle, 111, 113

Exceeding, 113
Explosion hazards, 28, 29
Eye-Ease drops, 102

Face and eye protection, 31, 32
Fire extinguishers, 22, 33
Fire-resistant metal cabinets, 23
First-aid kits, 32
Flame, types, 70
Flammables, 27
  Storing, 30
Flux core arc welding (FCAW), 106
  Switching to, 108, 109
Fluxes, 122, 135
  Mil-specs, 137
Fumes, 33, 92
Fusion welding with gas, 75–78
  Aluminum, 78, 79
  Stainless steel, 79

Gas brazing, 74, 75
Gas metal arc welding (GMAW), 105
Gas torch soldering and welding, 72
Gas welding, 34–36, 71
  Aluminum, hints, 80
  Steel, practicing, 80
Gases, 134
  Recommendations, 141
Goggles, 72, 73, 75

Hand tools, 24
Harbor Freight, 124
Hard facing,
  Implements, 102
  Plowshares, 101
  Steel, with gas, 79
  Rod to steel, 92
Harris Company, 118

Helium, 134, 141
Hobart Electric, 25, 130
Holes, drilling/piercing in steel, 119
Home Depot, 124, 133
Honda pressure washer, 24
Horseshoeing, 12, 13, 23
Hydrogen, 134, 141
Hydro-tested cylinders, 129

Iron Age, 9

JB Weld, 120, 122

Kohler generator, 18

Lincoln Electric, 25
Lowe's, 124

Mac tools, 24
Mail order welding supplies, 127
MAPP gas, 60
Mercury, 9
Metal cleaner, 140
Metal joining products, other, 122
Metals
  Hard-to-weld, 114–122
  Heating, 52, 53
  Identifying, 49–51
  Preparing for welding, 49
  Sources, 136
MIG welding, 38–40, 103–113
  Adjusting wire roller, 106
  Extension cords, 109, 110
  Hints, 112
  Making a good weld, 108
  Power voltage variation, 110
  Process, 39, 40
  Size, 105
  Spool guns, 111
  Techniques, 109
  Wire, 139
Miller Electric, 25
Models
  100-volt arc welding machine, 131
  110-volt arc welding machine, 99
  125-amp MIG welder, 103
  175-amp MIG welder, 23
  200-amp MIG welder, 23
  205-amp inverter-powered stick and TIG
    welder, 44

225-amp Lincoln buzzbox stick-welding machine, 24
250-ampHobart wire-feed welder, 24
BernzOmatic MAPP gas and oxygen torch, 21
Dillon pistol-grip torch and cutting head, 21
Harris model 15-3 aircraft welder, 69
Harris torch and cutting head, 21
Hobart MIG welder, 106
Lincoln 175-amp machine, 116
Lincoln 205-T, 85
Lincoln Electric Plasma 25 cutter machine, 62
Lincoln Electric Pro-Cut 25, 63
Lincoln Invertec V205T AC/DC TIG/Stick machine, 21, 81
Lincoln plasma torch, 65
Lincoln Pro-Cut 25 plasma cutting machine, 67, 68
Lincoln SP-125 PLUS welder, 104
Lincoln Square Wave 175 TIG/Stick machine, 17, 21
Lincoln TIG 175-amp welding machine, 114
Lincoln welders, 128
Lincoln Wisconsin V-4-powered, 81
Millenium MIG Spoolmate, 111
Miller 175-amp MIG welder, 108, 109
Miller Bobcat 225-amp gasoline-driven welder/generator, 23, 94
Miller plasma cutter, 68
Miller stick welder, 24
   Miller welders, 128
Miller wire-feel machine, 68
Millermatic 175-amp machine, 104
   Oxyacetylene welding set, 56
   Smiths aircraft torch, 21
   SP-125 Plus MIG welder, 21
   SP-125 welder, 105
Molybdenum, 9
Multiple passes, 101, 102

Neutral flame, 70
Nuts and bolts, 133

Overhead welding, 88, 94
Oxidizing flame, 70
Oxyacetylene, 36
   Rig, 17, 23
   Tanks, 56
Oxyacetylene cutting torch, 54–62
   Handles and torches, 61
   Operating, troubleshooting, 60, 61

Operation, 54
   Problems, troubleshooting, 61
   Shutting off, 58, 59
   Tips, 55
Oxyacetylene welding, 69–80
Oxygen, 134, 141
   Regulator, 56, 57

Parkinson's Disease, 92
Pastes for weld protection, 140
Phone, shopping by, 137
Pipe welding, 88
Plasma cutting 63–68
   Equipment, 40, 41, 43, 46
   Process, 43
   Operation, 65
   Troubleshooting, 65
Poly-Quick Stick, Cronatron, 120–122
Practice welding, 87
Preheating metals, 96
Propane gas, 60
Pro-Tools pipe and tubing bender, 25

Rods
   6011, 49
   Buying, 127, 129
   Cheap rods, 129, 132
   Copper-coated, 132
   Cronatron 321, 49
   Cronacast 211, 96, 116, 117, 119
   Cronacut Eagle 1100, 96, 114, 116–119
   Cronawear 79, 80
   Cronawear Eagle 7355, 92
   Cronaweld 333, 118, 119
   Cronaweld 510, 115, 118
   Cronaweld Eagle 3880, 119
   Dirty metal, 49
   E-6010, 85
   E-6011, 81, 84, 85, 97
   E-6013, 83, 85, 89–91
   E-6024, 84
   E-7018, 81, 83–85
   EasyStrike, MG Industries, 89
   Expensive commercial grade, 133, 134
   Jet Rod, 89
   Ni-Rod, 96, 119
   Numbers, 84
   Ovens, 85
   Polarity, 83
   Sizes and types, 81, 83–85
   Special types, 89
   Suggestions for stock, 85, 139, 140
   Rosebud tips, 63

Operating, 63

Safety, 27–33
Sandblasting cabinets, 22
Sanding disc, 24
Sears, 24, 124, 130, 131
Sheet metal, buying, 47, 48
Snap-on tools, 24
Solar Flux, 79
Solder, high-strength/low-temp, 120, 121
Solder, suggested supplies, 140
Soldering with gas, 70, 74
Solvent part washer, 24
Spark containment, 27–29
Specialty shops, 127
Stainless steel, 9
Steel, 34
   Angle, 48
   Buying, 47
   Metallurgy, 52, 53
Supply stores, 124

Types, 9
   Companies, 135–137
   Recommended, 138–141
   Steel Age, 9
   Storage racks, 48, 49
   Supplies
   Where to buy, 123–138
Tanks, transporting, 28, 29
Temperature, interpass, 102
Thin to thick metal welding, 90, 92
Tip cleaners, 73, 75
Tool steels, 9
Tools, 20–26
Tractor Supply Company, 124
Tungsten, 9

Vertical welding, 88, 90, 95
Vise-grip pliers, 91

Warpage, controlling, 90
Weather protection, 47
Welding area, cleaning, 31
Welding supply stores, 123, 124
Workshops, types, 15–19
Wire-feed welding, 38, 39
Wrenches, gas vs. oxy, 45

The Best Tools for the Job.

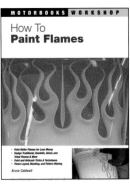

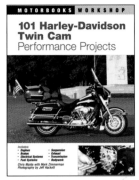

Other Great Books in this Series

Performance Welding Handbook
2nd Edition
0-7603-2172-8 • 139436AP

How To Paint Flames
0-7603-1824-7 • 137414AP

How To Build
Vintage Hot Rod V-8 Engines
0-7603-2084-5 • 138703AP

Honda & Acura
Performance Handbook
2nd Edition
0-7603-1780-1 • 137410AP

Hot Rod
Horsepower Handbook
0-7603-1814-X • 137220AP

How To Build the Cars of
The Fast and the Furious
0-7603-2077-2 • 138696AP

How To Tune and Modify Engine Man-
agement Systems
0-7603-1582-5 • 136272AP

Corvette Performance
Projects 1968–1982
0-7603-1754-2 • 137230AP

Custom Pickup Handbook
0-7603-2180-9 • 139348AP

Circle Track Chassis
& Suspension Handbook
0-7603-1859-X • 138626AP

How To Build A West Coast
Chopper Kit Bike
0-7603-1872-7 • 137253

101 Harley-Davidson Twin-Cam
Performance Projects
0-7603-1639-2 • 136265AP

101 Harley-Davidson
Performance Projects
0-7603-0370-3 • 127165AP

How To Custom Paint Your Motorcycle
0-7603-2033-0 • 138639AP

101 Sportbike Performance Projects
0-7603-1331-8 • 135742AP

Motorcycle Fuel Injection Handbook
0-7603-1635-X • 136172AP

ATV Projects: Get the Most Out
of Your All-Terrain Vehicle
0-7603-2058-6 • 138677AP

Four Wheeler
Chassis & Suspension Handbook
0-7603-1815-8 • 137235

Ultimate Boat
Maintenance Projects
0-7603-1696-1 • 137240AP

Motocross & Off-Road
Performance Handbook
3rd Edition
0-7603-1975-8 • 137408AP

How To Restore Your
Wooden Runabout
0-7603-1100-5 • 135107AP

Ultimate Garage Handbook
0-7603-1640-6 • 137389AP

How To Restore John Deere
Two-Cylinder Tractors
0-7603-0979-5 • 134861AP

How To Restore Your Farm Tractor
2nd Edition
0-7603-1782-8 • 137246AP

Mustang 5.0
Performance Projects
0-7603-1545-0 • 137245AP